Sustainable Housing
Principles & Practice

Contents

Contents

The authors

Hilary Armstrong is Minister of State at the Department of the Environment, Transport and the Regions, with responsibility for local government and regional planning. She is a member of the Cabinet Committee examining welfare reform and has overall responsibility for social exclusion and neighbourhood renewal. She is Member of Parliament for Durham West.

Chiel Boonstra trained as an architect at Delft University. He currently specialises in green issues in construction working with W/E Consultants in Gouda, The Netherlands. He is joint author of the book Handbook of Sustainable Building, published by James and James.

Edward Cullinan trained as an architect at Cambridge University, the Architectural Association in London and at the University of California, Berkeley. On graduating he worked for Denys Lasdun, forming his own practice in 1965 on co-operative principles. He has practised widely, winning many awards (including a CBE) for his distinctive organic approach to design.

Ben Derbyshire trained as an architect at Cambridge University joining Hunt Thompson Associates (now HTA) in 1976, becoming a partner in 1986. He is active in ensuring that resident participation is to the forefront of the design process. Besides leading the consortium that won the Greenwich Millennium Village project, he is on the Board of the Prince's Trust and a Fellow of the Royal Society of Arts.

Brian Edwards is Professor of Architecture at the University of Huddersfield. He has authored three books on green issues in building design, including Green Buildings Pay. He studied architecture and urban design at Canterbury, Edinburgh and Glasgow universities, gaining his PhD from the Mackintosh School of Architecture. With David Turrent he serves on the RIBA's Sustainabe Futures Committee.

Andrew Grant studied landscape architecture at Heriot-Watt University in Edinburgh forming his own practice in 1995. He previously worked for Battle McCarthy and Nicholas Pearson Associates. He collaborated with Richard Rogers on the Greenwich masterplan and for clients such as the Peabody Trust and John Makepeace. He is currently the masterplanner for the Earth Centre near Doncaster.

David Howarth studied engineering at Birmingham University gaining his PhD from the University of Manchester. He previously worked for North West Water and the National Rivers Authority. He is currently Project Leader and Manager of the Environment Agency's National Water Demand Management Centre.

David Lock is Visiting Professor of Town Planning at the University of Central England and Vice Chair of the Town and Country Planning Association. From 1994–97 he was Chief Planning Adviser to the Department of the Environment and is Managing Director of David Lock Associates – a practice specialising in planning and urban design.

George Mills studied architecture at Huddersfield University, setting up the architectural practice of Mills, Beaumont, Leavey and Channon in Manchester in the early 1980s. His practice has undertaken major urban renewal projects in Manchester, Newcastle and Paris. At Hulme, where the practice has worked since 1991, MBLC has developed a new approach to inner city regeneration which links the civic realm to sustainability.

Peter F. Smith is Professor of Architecture at Sheffield Hallam University. From 1989–97 he chaired the RIBA's Energy and Environment Committee and was the organiser of several important conferences on sustainable design. He studied architecture at Cambridge University, gaining his PhD from the University of Manchester. He has authored widely on green issues in building design. He currently chairs the RIBA's Sustainable Futures Committee.

Derek Taylor studied architecture at the Architectural Association, has a Masters degree in industrial design engineering from the Royal College of Art and a PhD from the Open University. He is principal of Altechnica,

a multidisciplinary practice specialising in renewable energy design and development.

David Turrent studied architecture at Manchester University and has since specialised in low energy housing design. He was a founding partner of ECD Architects and has been responsible for several award winning projects including 'Green Building of the Year'. He is a member of the RIBA's Sustainabe Futures Committee and also serves on the Construction Industry Council's (CIC) Environment Committee.

Andrew Wright is an architect having worked for eight years for the Richard Rogers Partnership before setting up his own practice. In 1994 he won first prize for architecture at the Royal Academy for his design for a Buddhist retreat on Holy Island. Andrew Wright Associates specialises in low energy design and is involved in developing sustainability guidelines for the DETR.

Acknowledgements

The editors and authors wish to record their appreciation of the Royal Institute of British Architects who organised the conference upon which this book is based, the Building Research Establishment who provided courteous and prompt replies to queries, the DETR for their many helpful publications and the Joseph Rowntree Foundation for its conference sponsorship. In addition, many practices have provided drawings and photographs which confirm the aesthetic as well as environmental benefits of sustainable design.

A particular debt is due to those who tirelessly typed and corrected the many manuscripts, particularly Karen Beaumont and the staff of Academic Typing Services at the University of Huddersfield.

Finally, the editors wish to place on record their debt to the individual chapter authors for their unbounded helpfulness and enthusiasm in the face of countless faxes, letters, telephone calls and e-mails.

Picture credits

The authors and the publishers would like to thank the following individuals and organisations for permission to reproduce material. We have made every effort to contact and acknowledge copyright holders, but if any errors have been made we would be happy to correct them at a later printing.

Photographers

Martin Charles F3
All other photographs by Brian Edwards

Individuals and organisations

Andrew Wright 8.1, 8.2, 8.4, 8.6, 8.7, 8.8, 8.9, 8.10
BP Solar 13.9
BRECSU 13.6
Building Research Establishment 1.10, 1.13
Cartwright Pickard 1.17
Cole Thompson 13.7
CZWG 1.28
David Turrent 12.7
Derek Taylor 4.1, 4.2, 4.4, 4.5, 4.6, 4.7
DETR 1.6
DLA 2.5, 2.7, 2.8, 2.9, 2.10
ECD Architects 12.2, 12.5, 12.6
Edward Cullinan 11.1, 11.2, 11.3, 11.4, 11.5, 11.6, 11.7, 11.8
Environment Agency 5.2, 5.3, 5.5, 5.6, 5.7

George Mills 10.2, 10.3
Gil Schalom/Chris Madden/The Guardian 13.15
Grant Associates 3.3
Hackland Dove Architects 1.8
Hunt Thompson Associates 9.1, 9.3, 9.4, 9.5, 9.6, 9.7
Joost Brouwers 6.4, 6.5
Julyan Wickham 13.2
Krister Wiberg 1, 12.3, 13.1, 13.8
London Docklands Development Corporation 1.25, 1.27, 3.1
Levitt Bernstein 1.5, 13.10
Manchester Library Services 10.1
Martin Richardson 2
Michael Squire 1.2, 1.26
Mills Beaumont Leavey Channon 10.4, 10.5, 10.6, 10.8, 10.9, 10.10
Murray O'Laoire 13.5
North British Housing Association 10.7
NOVEM 1.16, 6.1, 6.2, 6.3
Price & Cullen 2.3
Ralph Erskine 9.1, 9.2, 9.3, 9.4, 9.5, 9.6, 9.7
REAG 4.3
Richard Parnaby 2.6
Susan Pritchard 2.4
Western Isles Island Council 13.3

Foreword
Sustainability and housing: the government view

HILARY ARMSTRONG

What is sustainable housing?

Housing is an important element in this government's broad social agenda. It overlaps with employment, health, education, crime and many other aspects of people's lives. It is key, therefore, to our strategy for tackling social exclusion and achieving our targets for sustainable development. One look at the remit of the Prime Minister's Social Exclusion Unit – where deprived neighbourhoods and rough sleeping feature as two of the three priority areas for early action – should be enough to demonstrate the importance that we attach to housing.

We are committed to securing improvements in the quality of housing and housing management and are making available an extra £5 billion within the lifetime of this parliament for investment in housing to raise standards. But equally important, our housing policy is about making sure people belong. It is about enabling people to have a decent quality of life, involving them and giving them control over how they live. Our aim overall, is to offer everyone the opportunity of a decent home and so promote social cohesion, well-being and self-dependence.

What, then, are our specific policies on *sustainable* housing? In the broadest sense, I think I have already described them. Sustainable housing should ensure a better quality of life, not just now but for future generations as well. It should combine protection of the environment, sensible use of natural resources, economic growth and social progress.

Social progress is an important factor, which I believe has been left off the sustainable housing agenda too often in the past. Sustainability should encompass not just the

1 Improvement to the quality and management of existing housing is a key aspect of government policy for social sustainability.

fabric of buildings – although that is important – but also what I call the 'people factor'. Housing is sustainable if everyone has the opportunity of access to a home that is decent; if it promotes social cohesion, well-being and self-dependence. That is our aim.

Building sustainable communities

The government is revising the national Sustainable Development Strategy (now published). Our consultation document on this, *Opportunities for Change*, introduced

social progress as a key element in sustainable development. It specifically asked people what they thought helped to build sustainable communities. We received a large and encouraging response to this section of the consultation. What came out most strikingly was the desire of people to play a part in shaping their communities. They wanted greater community empowerment and local accountability given to the community.

Architects, house builders, local authorities, housing associations, lenders and others involved in providing housing have a key role to play in promoting developments that will sustain communities. The construction, design, location and mix of tenure and type of housing can all be critical to the long term quality of life for the communities who will live there, including energy use and environmental impact.

But we must all make greater efforts to build community consultation and participation into all stages of the development process – from drawing up plans to handing over keys, and beyond. If people are given a sense of ownership – a feeling that they belong and are part of the community, able to contribute to decisions affecting their lives and the lives of their families, friends and neighbours – communities will become more sustainable.

'Best Value' – the new duty we will be placing on local authorities to secure the services the public want at the price they are prepared to pay – will increase local accountability. It will bring new challenges and opportunities in terms of service delivery and tenant involvement. If 'Best Value' is going to work, tenants and residents must be involved from the start – influencing service planning and delivery, and ensuring that standards are met.

Effective tenant participation is one of the keys to strengthening and building sustainable communities. That is why the government wants to see tenant participation compacts established between local authority landlords and their tenants. The compacts will set out minimum expectations for empowering tenants and codify the rights and responsibilities of tenants and the authority in establishing arrangements for participation. They will be underpinned by good practice guidance.

A key aspect in building sustainable communities is ensuring that housing is built in the right place. In February 1998 the Deputy Prime Minister announced our new strategy for accommodating future demand for housing. The aim is to promote more sustainable patterns of development by making better use of our towns and cities, making them more attractive and so reducing the need for development to spread into the countryside. Better integration with transport is the key to building sustainable communities.

Recently, my department published the government's response to the report of the House of Commons Select Committee inquiry into these issues. We very much wel-come the Committee's endorsement of our 60% target for building new housing on previously used land. However, building more on brownfield land rather than using up the resource of greenfields is only a start. In order to develop or recover expertise about how to create sustainable communities we are about to publish a guide to *Planning for Sustainable Development* [now published]. But it is far from the last word on this subject. There is a huge new area being opened up for planners and architects about what design and planning for sustainable communities actually means, how it is to be achieved, and how communities are to be involved.

We are actively putting in place some of the mechanisms required to enhance sustainable communities – for example by reviewing planning guidance on housing, transport and recreation – but we need a wider debate on what the sustainable built environment actually entails. I believe architects and planners ought to be at the forefront of that debate and I invite you to take up the challenge.

An urban renaissance

In launching the prospectus of the Urban Task Force in 1998, the Deputy Prime Minister spoke about his vision for an Urban Renaissance. It is an aspiration that all of us in government share. For too long our cities have been characterised as ghettos of social exclusion, often lacking even the most basic facilities. Dirty, polluted by traffic jams, noisy and unattractive, with poor standards of housing. Communities are too often divided by fear rather than united by common causes. That is why we believe an Urban Renaissance is needed with consequent changes in ideas, in perceptions and in the physical environment. It means good design – creating buildings and an urban environment that people enjoy living in, working in, and visiting.

One aspect of that vision will be the creation of urban villages. These are not intended as blueprints. Local circumstances are unique and developments need to reflect the needs of the local community. The aim is to promote living and sustainable communities, not 'model villages', and to test them through actual development in different parts of the country. For example, the 32 acre

2 *The redevelopment of a brownfield site in central Glasgow for student housing. Integrated transport will help us return streets to communities.*
Architect: GRM Kennedy and Partners

Millennium Village is about to be built on a very large brownfield site on the Greenwich Peninsula. This will be a flagship urban development scheme, an example of what urban living in the next century could be about. The Village will create an enduring legacy for the future and is only a part of the wider millennium project for regenerating the whole Peninsula. The Millennium Village, and other urban villages such as Allerton Bywater near Leeds, will provide important lessons for sustainable development.

These projects are one element of what the government sees as a wider cultural shift. There are undoubted obstacles to be overcome, but the greatest of these is perception. We must all work hard to implement change. The more people become aware of the benefits to be achieved, the more expectations can be raised. The more that we can point to schemes that have been successfully implemented, then the greater the changes that can be made.

New Deal for Communities

We must not, in our enthusiasm for new development in the next millennium, forget the legacy of the past. There is too much housing in this country that is in poor condition or located in areas of multiple deprivation. I have already mentioned the additional £5 billion for investment in housing. This will help to improve the condition of our existing housing stock, providing benefits for health and the environment. As a result of our Comprehensive Spending Review in 1998, we also announced a £3 billion regeneration package over the next three years to tackle the problems of the most deprived areas. The government recognises the importance of stabilising and empowering communities for their own renewal. There will, as a start, be £800 million of new money over the next three years to begin to tackle the most acute examples of deprived neighbourhoods, through the New Deal for Communities.

As a mark of our commitment to innovation, we are determined to develop new types of partnerships to lead neighbourhood renewal. Organisations such as community groups and housing associations are being encouraged to actively participate and lead pathfinder projects. The New Deal for Communities is about more than just renewing estates requiring regeneration. It is about empowering people excluded from influence; providing chances for people denied both opportunity and choice; about bringing hope to areas where hopelessness and desolation have run riot. That is why we are saying to each of the pathfinder areas: involve and empower the residents; address the fundamentals; think afresh and from first principles, work from the bottom up; form new partnerships, find radical, exciting, sustainable solutions.

Housing and health

Sustainable communities also need to be healthy communities. We recognise that there are associations between poor housing and health – particularly links between cold and damp housing and physical well-being. In recognition of these links we have commissioned work to develop and test a fitness rating to replace the current housing fitness standard. The new fitness rating will encompass the impor-

3 *Good design is crucial to the creation of urban environments that people enjoy living in. Architect: Jeremy Dixon/BDP*

tant health and safety risks in the home and distinguish between the varying severity of those risks. As such it should provide a more effective mechanism for identifying and targeting action on the worst housing. Our target is to have a finalised rating scheme by July 1999 and to seek a suitable legislative slot for its introduction as soon as possible thereafter. But the government is not just introducing a new measure of what is unfit. The substantial additional resources we have made available for housing and regeneration will lead to real improvements in the condition of the stock overall and in the surrounding environment.

Energy efficiency

Good energy efficient homes provide better environments for people living in them as well as reducing the impact on the natural environment. Currently the domestic sector accounts for nearly 26% of our carbon dioxide emissions – some 41 million tonnes of carbon – much of it through heating. It is essential that we take steps to reduce these emissions both through improved new designs and also by tackling existing housing that has poor energy efficiency.

We are carrying out a comprehensive review of the Building Regulations to see how their contribution to the government's carbon dioxide targets can be maximised. The review is addressing all types of buildings, considering both housing and commercial properties. As well as covering how standards for new construction could be raised, the possibilities for capturing more repair and maintenance work in the existing stock of buildings and for controlling the performance of buildings in use are also being investigated.

Local authorities with housing responsibilities are required by the Home Energy Conservation Act to identify energy conservation measures for residential accommodation in their area. Much of the additional money made available for investment in housing will lead to energy efficiency improvements. There is a range of other measures we are taking, including the promotion of energy services packages, community heating schemes (particularly those using combined heat and power technology) and, through the Energy Saving Trust, public education and the promotion of energy efficient products. We are also tackling fuel poverty through our Home Energy Efficiency Scheme, with investment of some £375 million over the next three years.

Transport

Transport has a major impact on carbon dioxide emissions and on the sustainability of housing and communities. If we are serious about sustainable development we must be serious about transport policy; about tackling congestion and reducing pollution. I mentioned earlier the importance of better integration between transport and the location of new housing developments. As John Prescott said in 1998 when the *Integrated Transport* White Paper was launched, 'doing nothing is not an option'.

The emphasis in the White Paper is on a package of measures that make up a New Deal for Transport. There is no one 'big idea' to solve all the problems associated with transport, health and the environment; instead the White Paper challenges all of us to act: central government, local government, planners, transport providers, industry and everyone who travels. We must all do our bit to find solutions that are tailored to local circumstances.

Integrated transport is a long term agenda and one that is fundamental to the creation and survival of sustainable communities. How we move around within and between our communities affects our health, our children's education and our social development. Good urban design is crucial to integrating transport, development, social and environmental factors.

Housing Quality Indicators

With such a wide range of issues to consider, we need to develop new, flexible tools to help us assess the quality of housing, and ensure that it provides value for money. Earlier attempts to establish quality thresholds in housing, like the old Parker Morris standards, concentrated on a limited range of physical benchmarks. Important as these were, we now need to develop a much more comprehensive approach that scores housing on its overall quality.

That is why we have published a set of Housing Quality Indicators, which can be used to evaluate all the factors that are crucial to the design of high quality sustainable housing; from location, layout and space standards, to maintenance and energy use in both construction and running costs. The initial impetus for the research that led to their development came from the Housing Group at the RIBA.

Although the Housing Quality Indicators will initially be used by the DETR and the Housing Corporation to evaluate the quality of publicly funded housing, we believe that they have considerable potential for use in the private sector as well. I hope that architects, planners and house builders will work with us to develop and refine the Indicators as a measurement tool which both developers and consumers can use for guidance.

In conclusion, there is a wide range of issues that affect the sustainability of housing, many of which will feature in the government's revised Sustainable Development Strategy. We all need to consider these issues and the part we can play in ensuring that the combination of our activities adds up to environmental, economic and social progress – to sustainable housing and to sustainable communities.

Hilary Armstrong,
Minister for Local Government and the Regions

Introduction
Sustainable housing

BRIAN EDWARDS

The creation of low energy, ecological housing has become a key component of sustainable development. Living in harmony with the environment has become an essential component of the design of homes and neighbourhoods in the third millennium. The Labour government, reversing Conservative party policy, is grappling with the triple imperatives of expanding housing provision, bringing back into use 'brownfield' land, whilst also reducing atmospheric carbon emissions. We have, as a society, moved fairly rapidly from an understanding of sustainable development to framing policies in a wide range of secondary fields from sustainable construction to integrated transportation. Housing, which is responsible for 27% of all CO_2 emissions in the UK, has a key role to play in helping us fashion more sustainable lifestyles.

There are a number of different perspectives on sustainable housing and each is subject to distinct design parameters. More than practically any other building type, housing encompasses technical, social, political and economic issues. Designers, developers and housing managers face serious obstacles to attaining sustainable housing, yet the pressure and opportunities are greater than at any time in the past. More sustainable patterns of housing based upon enhanced environmental and energy performance will need to become mainstream if sustainable development is to be achieved across the country. Design is the key to unlocking the potential of the new energy and ecological awareness, giving architects a greatly expanded role in the field of volume housing.

Over the past decade the emphasis has shifted from the low energy house to the environmentally sustainable neighbourhood. The individual dwelling is important but

Sustainable housing

1 *Good urban design is essential if sustainable communities are to be created.*
Architect: Martin Richardson

the main benefit lies in tackling volume housing and existing urban areas. Various observers have noted the importance of relating questions of sustainability to wider problems of poverty, unemployment and social exclusion. The run-down inner city or peripheral estate is likely not only to be energy inefficient but the inhabitants may also be suffering from high levels of sickness, drug or alcohol abuse, poor education levels, social division and unemployment. Sustainable housing cannot ignore these problems and many of the examples in this book illustrate how they may be overcome by new approaches to the design of neighbourhoods.

If perceptions of sustainability have moved from the individual building to the estate, it has seen a shift also in the way multi-sector solutions are now necessary. Transportation and urban form are seen today as essential elements of any strategy for sustainable housing. With the broadening of interest comes the need to integrate action – to develop holistic models for living, working and leisure. So, whereas a decade or two ago architects and engineers developed prototypes of the autonomous house, today effort is directed towards the self sustaining community. The culmination of this process are developments such as Ecolonia in The Netherlands, Findhorn in Scotland and the ambitious plans for the Greenwich Millennium Village discussed later in this book.

The green context

Chapter 1

Sustainable housing: architecture, society and professionalism

BRIAN EDWARDS

No society is balanced and in harmony with nature unless housing is sustainable. Housing, as against individual houses, is central to perceptions of quality of life; attractive homes in well managed estates are as important as education and job security to urban satisfaction. Professional institutes have a duty to serve society in the provision of decent housing. This means housing that is desirable, well maintained, free of crime and of low energy design.

The provision of sustainable housing is fundamentally about the design and management of the housing stock. A decent home is essential for social cohesion, personal well-being and self-dependence. Housing impacts upon quality of life issues far more than any other form of architecture. The professions, particularly the RIBA, have played a large part in creating innovative, socially responsive housing in the past. Sustainability provides the impetus to give this inheritance a fresh cutting edge.

There is little genuine social progress without good quality housing. Housing is at the root of cultural and economic vitality because it is the agent that cements communities. The professions have been responsible for some of the finest and worst housing in the UK this century: urban housing that on some occasions has uplifted community spirit and on others damped it down.

It is one thing to design the fabric of buildings, quite another to sustain the fabric of communities through good environmental design. Architects, however, need to realise that buildings alone do not make sustainable neighbourhoods. There are areas outside the architects' control that are equally important: road or estate layout; landscape design; density; and housing type. These are also areas outside the developers' control: social mix; employment opportunities; and quality of schools. No matter how

1.1 *Housing is essential to quality of life. This example of mixed tenure, mixed income housing in London Docklands is designed by Pinchin Kellow.*

beautiful or low in energy usage the design may be, the creation of sustainable housing requires team effort and the ethos of partnership.

The government paper *Opportunities for Change*, published in 1998, signals the importance of social progress in attaining 'sustainable development'. Architects and developers are encouraged to listen to tenants and owner occupiers when housing briefs are being drawn up. The concerns of tenants – crime, job opportunities, heating bills, rubbish and vandalism – are rarely heeded by those who design or manage estates. *Opportunities for Change* suggests that the ownership of '*sustainable housing*' must reside in people and tenant groups, not housing providers and their professional advisers. The split between social and private housing does not remove the obligation to talk to those whose communities are being fashioned by designers and developers. Local accountability is the first principle of sustainable housing and professional practices must learn to put the community first – not profit, fees or speed of construction. In theory, local accountability should provide the basis for decisions on design, construction method and layout as well as tenure mix, management and crime prevention strategy.

The professions need to ensure that the 4.1 million new homes expected to be created by 2016 are in the right place, of the right type and well integrated with public transport. Location and design are the two key aspects of sustainable housing. New development is not sustainable if it is remote from transport connections and requires private forms of transport to join it to the fabric of society – jobs, shopping, leisure, schools. In fact, it is no longer ethical to engage in such housing given the international and national obligations towards sustainable development. It is also professionally unacceptable to design housing that is energy inefficient, encourages crime, does not provide for disabled access and ignores opportunities for recycling of waste or water.

Housing, employment, education and leisure should not be separately zoned activities but integrated into attractive mixed use neighbourhoods. Physical separation has to be replaced by social integration – this is the second principle of sustainability. With integration will come improved levels of energy efficiency because compact

Table 1.1 Options for meeting 4.1 million new households by 2016

– brownfield site redevelopment (50%)	
– outward growth at urban periphery	Remaining 50%
– greater intensification of suburbs	
– new settlements in countryside	

Source: Sustainable Settlements and Shelter, HMSO, 1997

Table 1.2 Advantages by recycling brownfield sites

- reduces pressure on undeveloped land, especially green belts
- improves viability of public transport
- raises density of cities thereby utilising infrastructure better
- assists social and economic regeneration
- enhances appearance and image of towns

Source: Adapted from Planning for Sustainable Development: Towards Better Practice, HMSO, 1998

development allows heat loss from one building to be the heat gain for another. Compaction, high density, connection and liveability are held in mutually supporting cycles of sustainable benefit.

The government's target of building 60% of new housing on existing developed land has several benefits for society and the design professions. For society, the preservation of green belt land helps preserve an agricultural and leisure resource for the future. Towns that do not coalesce into others keep their identity and this helps maintain social or community fabric. The professions benefit from brownfield site development because of the new specialist skills required – in site reclamation, in designing for the remediation of contamination, and in creating solutions on difficult parcels of land. Dealing with pollution, waste and recycling demands knowledge and skill of a high order. So

1.2 *Density is a prerequisite for sustainable housing. Sufferance Quay in London Docklands by Michael Squire Associates on brownfield land.*

The green context

1.3 *Robust social housing on brownfield land in central Glasgow. Architect: Glasgow City Council*

1.4 *Compact mixed use housing on brownfield land in the centre of San Francisco. We need to learn from international example.*

much new housing of recent years has been built on greenfield land that, although developers and architects are accomplished at the design of suburban estates, they have lost the knack of creating human-scaled urban development. There are exceptions – Byker in Newcastle, some areas of London Docklands, the Merchant City in Glasgow – but generally the inner city has suffered as developers have targeted the urban fringe.

Too many inner city neighbourhoods are today blighted by traffic, with polluted air and water, and divided by fear. Sustainable development offers the prospect of clean, healthy neighbourhoods as long as government, the professions and the building industry rise to the challenge. The urban renaissance brought about by the concept of sustainable development will change practice throughout the industry but it will take time to evolve new models of urban housing, new patterns of integrating living and working, and new ways of using urban design to achieve social integration.

Urban villages are part of the answer but it is important that the suburbanisation of the inner city – so prevalent in Liverpool – is avoided. Compact forms of living, common in France, The Netherlands, Germany and Scotland, are not part of the English way of life. Architects can lead the change in taste by using good design and demonstration projects to signal the cultural shift in favour of sustainability. Work by Urban Splash, the development company based in Manchester, points in the right direction.

The perception of sustainable housing remains a problem. Too often we have good sustainable housing in poor positions and poor housing in good positions. Since housing produces 27% of all CO_2 emissions, generating 45 million tonnes of atmospheric carbon per year, it is important that we address residential energy consumption as a priority. The government's crusade to raise urban densities is part of the answer. The DETR report *Planning for Sustainable Development* suggests that housing densities

1.5 *Inner city housing in Leeds for the Joseph Rowntree Foundation designed by Levitt Bernstein (perspective and plan).*

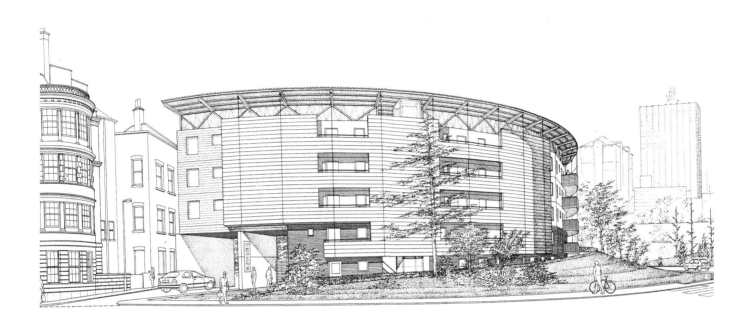

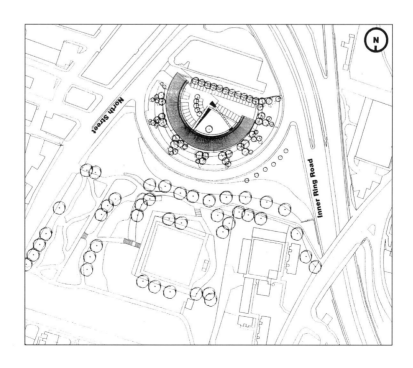

1.6 *Emissions of greenhouse gases in UK. Source: Sustainability Counts, HMSO, 1998*

1.7 *Key interactions in climate change. Brian Edwards BRE*

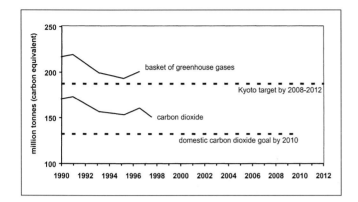

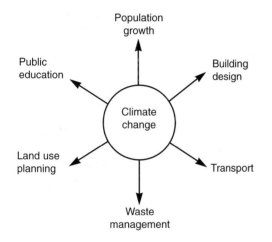

to be damaging to the surrounding townscape, much of it adjoining a conservation area.

Health and energy are related concerns of sustainable housing. Sustainability provides the principles upon which healthy, comfortable, hopeful communities are created. However, as the existing building stock is replaced at under 1% per year, we need to address the present infrastructure of housing with as much enthusiasm as new construction. Unfortunately, most effort is directed towards the design of new housing, not the upgrading of existing buildings. This is true of BRE advice, the Building Regulations and professional attention. It would be useful if more small extensions or alterations were controlled in order to extend the scope and impact of the Building Regulations, particularly to the DIY arena. So much small-scaled work (window replacement, conservatories, etc.) has doubtful energy benefit or is not cost effective against CO_2 emission savings.

Demonstration projects offer many advantages: they smooth changes in public opinion in favour of sustainability; they allow for the testing of new energy technologies; they provide the vehicle for developing novel design solutions. The DETR's recent announcement in the Urban Task Force report of a system of regional sustainable housing demonstration schemes is a welcome step forward. Sustainable development opens up fresh opportunities for designers. Government has a part to play, just as the Dutch one has done over the past decade, in encouraging or facilitating change. The future offers an expansion in demand for new energy services, in a fresh generation of environmental products and designs, in initiatives such as community based heating schemes (based upon CHP principles) and in new ways of harnessing renewable energy. These changes will bring in their wake expectations that only well skilled architects, engineers and developers can meet.

The 1990s have seen the strategy for sustainable development extended into specific policies for sustainable housing and sustainable construction. The first decade of the next millennium will see words turned into action. Architects will again have a key role to play in mass housing, but it is important that the mistakes of the 1960s are not repeated. Cost is not the same as value, speed of construction is only one measure of efficiency, factory

should rise significantly from around 120 habitable rooms per hectare (HRH) to 225–275 HRH. In some urban areas even densities approaching 1,000 HRH are possible, though taking other factors into account (such as crime, micro-climate and access) a norm of 500–550 is preferable. A recent scheme for the Peabody Trust in Islington highlights the difficulties of excessive density. With 750 HRH, the planning authority turned down the application although it was alongside a railway station and had as a consequence abandoned parking space for private cars. The council believed the scheme too dense, lacked amenity space and the high buildings (13 storeys) were thought

1.8 *Examples of sustainable urban housing are too frequently projects rather than built schemes. This design by Hackland Dove Architects is planned for the Gorgie area of Edinburgh.*

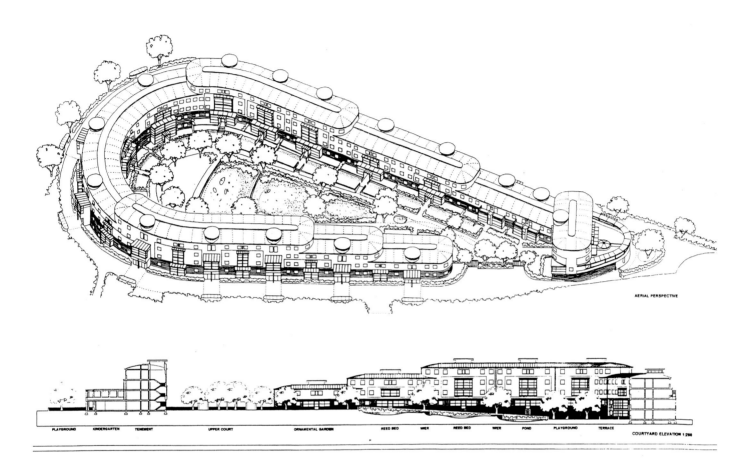

AERIAL PERSPECTIVE

PLAYGROUND   KINDERGARTEN   TENEMENT   UPPER COURT   ORNAMENTAL GARDEN   REED BED   WER   REED BED   WER   POND   PLAYGROUND   TERRACE
                                                                                                                                                        COURTYARD ELEVATION 1:250

production is not necessarily better, and finally, height is not the same thing as greater density. With sustainability as a guiding principle, architecture, society and professionalism could form a useful new ethical compact.

Towards a definition of sustainable housing

In the context of the UK, sustainable housing is as much a question of sustainable urban renewal as the creation of new sustainable communities. So many houses of doubtful quality have already been built, and so much urban land is derelict or degraded, that sustainability has necessarily to address existing residential areas as much as the design of new neighbourhoods. As a society we have yet to formulate a definition of sustainable housing, let alone sustainable urban renewal. A useful starting point is the Brundtland Commission definition of 1987 which describes sustainable development as 'development that meets the needs of the present without compromising the ability of future generations to meet their own needs' (see Table 13.1). The Brundtland approach is resource based, and this, because of the growing realisation of global warming, has increasingly been interpreted in the construction industry as a question of low energy design. However, energy efficiency is not the

1.9 *Concept diagram of sustainable development.*

1.10 *This comparison of energy use by house type (assuming equal floor area and orientation) shows the importance of density to sustainable development. BRE*

only issue with regard to housing, and for many tenants of social housing schemes, the priority is staying warm, living in safe neighbourhoods and keeping water bills down.

Although it is now widely known that buildings contribute half of the UK's total CO_2 emissions, it is less understood that they also generate 16% of the nation's waste during the construction stage. Housing generates a particularly large amount of this waste as a result of the packaging of many of the construction products. Where packaging is not a problem, the craft based industries of brickwork, plastering and decorating generate waste as a result of breakages or the cutting and mixing of materials on site. Typically also in the UK, households use 140 litres of water per person per day, a figure that is rising by 8% per year. It is clear from these figures released in 1998 by consulting engineers Oscar Faber, that construction has the single biggest contribution to make to sustainable development.

One may, therefore, define sustainable housing as 'housing that meets the perceived and real needs of the present in a resource efficient fashion whilst providing attractive, safe and ecologically rich neighbourhoods'. Resource efficient is not the same as zero impact but it does imply the Brundtland contract between current resource usage and future demand. Or put another way, the definition accepts a responsibility to create physical capital in the form of housing that represents a long term robust, yet flexible resource. Future generations will need their own supplies of energy but they need also the handing on of built assets of quality. This largely has been the problem of housing created over the past two generations – it has not represented (with certain exceptions) good intergenerational asset value.

Sustainability is a process; sustainable development is the product. The process must, in the field of housing, address five distinct fields:

* the conservation of natural resources (land, energy, water)
* the sensible re-use of man-made resources
* maintenance of ecosystems and their regenerative potential
* equity between generations, peoples and classes
* provision of health, safety and security.

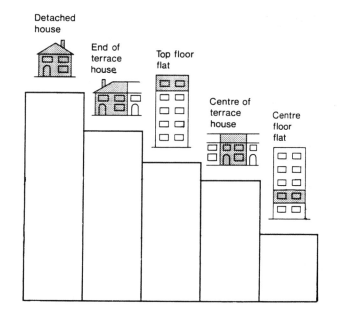

E₁ - Energy
E₂ - Environment
E₃ - Ecology
S₁ - Society
S₂ - Sustainability

Detached house
End of terrace house
Top floor flat
Centre of terrace house
Centre floor flat

Any national housing strategy or design of a sustainable community should, therefore, establish targets in these fields. The objective is, of course, to fashion housing developments that are valued by their communities (environmentally and aesthetically) whilst providing long term capital assets. To do the latter they will need to evolve through a process of neighbourhood participation with the design brief recognising social value as well as profit. The tools are well known but not always employed, and nature provides excellent examples of resource use, recycling and diversity.

Our five point priorities for sustainable housing

1.11 *These modest, low energy houses consume only half the energy of buildings equivalent. Giffard Park Housing Co-operative, Milton Keynes designed by ECD Architects*

place energy use within the first target. How much energy is used per household and per design type is central to any strategy for reducing carbon emissions. The international agreements reached at the Earth Summit at Rio in 1992 and strengthened by the Kyoto Conference on Climate Change in 1997 depend upon firm energy targets for housing. Since housing contributes 27% towards national CO_2 emissions in the UK, it is here that engineers, architects, clients and users need to focus their attention. A typical 1930s house in Britain produces 8 tonnes of CO_2 per year in heating and lighting, although this has been reduced to about 4 tonnes in 1998 through the evolution of better designs, higher insulation standards and the exploitation of renewable energy. Transport to and from housing contributes a further 4–5 tonnes of CO_2 per year, making housing design, housing layout and location key factors in meeting our international obligations.

Other resources besides energy

Energy is not, however, the only resource to consider. Domestic water consumption is becoming increasingly critical, especially in southern Britain. Changing patterns of rain-

Table 1.3 Carbon dioxide (CO_2) emissions by sector in UK

Transport	29.5
Housing	27.4
Industrial processes	23.1
Service sector	14.4
Other buildings	4.3
Other	1.3

Source: BRECSU, 1998

Table 1.4 Historical pattern of CO_2 emissions for typical house (semi-detached) per year

Year	Amount	Fuel source
1900	11 tonnes	(coal)
1930	8 tonnes	(coal)
1976	6 tonnes	(oil)
1990	5 tonnes	(gas)
1998	4 tonnes	(gas/electric)
2010	2 tonnes	(renewables/gas/electricity)

Source: BRE, EU and DETR

Table 1.5 Typical levels of CO_2 generation by the average family

New house built to modern Building Regulations	4¹/₄ tonnes/yr
Older house (pre 1960)	10 tonnes/yr
Family car use	4¹/₂ tonnes/yr
Family holiday to Mediterranean	2¹/₂ tonnes/yr
Family food	4 tonnes/yr

Source: Building Research Establishment, 1998

fall because of global warming, the over exploitation of ground water supplies through the proliferation of deep boreholes, the growth in households and of white goods means that water is increasingly seen as 'tomorrow's oil'. As with energy consumption, the level of water use is increasing nationally in spite of greater distribution efficiency as a result of growth in households. Typically today a new house has two, even three bathrooms, a power shower, dishwasher and washing machine. Domestic water consumption has increased by nearly 40% per household over the past 15 years. We may be cleaner and healthier but the global price has been high and if current levels of increase in water use continue, the UK will run out of water by 2012 and the European Union by 2008. Sustainable housing cannot therefore avoid the question of water efficiency.

Much the same principles apply to water as with energy conservation. Recycling loops need to be considered, using for example washing machine waste water for garden irrigation, and bath waste water for toilet flushing. In Britain very little rainwater striking the house is collected even for use in watering vegetables. Water conservation too is a question of reduced or more efficient use. Waterless toilet flushing is available, reduced flow taps with automatic cut off have been on the market for some time, and washing machines can be purchased with much lower levels of water use than a few years ago. Since about 40% of all water in the UK is consumed in dwellings, it is the home and how it is designed that should be at the centre of water conservation policies.

Energy and water are key resources but so too is land. Over the past 50 years, 80% of all land lost from agri-

Table 1.6 Water use in UK

Year	Amount	
1985	100 litres/person/day	Rising trend
2000	160 litres/person/day	

Source: Environment Agency, 1999

1.12 *Land, energy and built form are held in important circles of interdependency in terms of sustainability.*

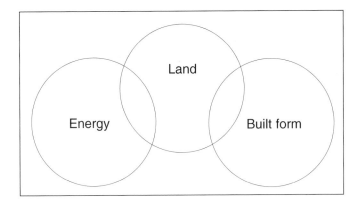

cultural production has been the result of urban settlement growth, much of it for housing. The housing created has often been low density and supported by other land consuming activities such as business parks, suburban retail areas and massive road construction. Suburban growth in detached and semi-detached houses consumes four times the land area per family housed as urban patterns of living (compact terraces and walk-up flats) with nearly three times the amount of energy per household (in space heating and transport). Resource conservation cannot be achieved without a fundamental review of the type, form and location of housing.

The land lost from agriculture this century is nearly 20% of the total productive land of the country. It has been estimated that even if all the agricultural land of England was employed, it could not today produce enough food to feed metropolitan London. Neither can all the woods of England absorb the CO_2 emitted by London.

Land lost from agriculture through development is rarely returned to productive use. Certainly some fruit and vegetables are grown in suburban gardens (and often greater biodiversity exists here than in agricultural areas), but efficient food production suffers as cities consume land directly and threaten other areas by planning ambition. Agricultural land produces food crops and has the potential to grow energy crops. Recently, the Ministry of Agriculture has encouraged the growing of biomass crops for use in digestion power stations or as domestic fuel. So as we lose land, the ability of future generations to grow

crops (both food and energy) is curtailed. This means importing food with further energy burdens in terms of CO_2 emissions. Whilst a typical house contributes 8 tonnes of carbon dioxide per year, and transport $4^1/2$ tonnes, food consumption represents a further 4–5 tonnes of CO_2 per household. Land, energy and built form are held in important circles of interdependency in terms of sustainability.

Embodied energy

Much recent research has explored the relationship between embodied energy and energy in use for typical building types and forms of construction. As a rule of thumb, embodied energy (i.e. the amount of energy required to construct the building) is less than 20% of full lifetime energy use. However, since housing tends to be a long surviving building type, the percentage can be under 10. Hence, it is important to concentrate upon energy performance in use, providing opportunities through good design for periodic upgrading to take advantage of technological innovation. This is why in certain housing projects described later (e.g. Greenwich Millennium Village) a distinction is made between permanent and renewable parts. The fixed parts are usually the main walls and structure and the flexible ones the building services. The space between walls and floors provides a zone of replaceability. This allows kitchens, bathrooms, water and heating services and insulation levels to be upgraded (according to taste and energy targets) whilst accepting the principal structural constraints of the building frame. Space too can be remodelled by the addition or subtraction of dividing walls, providing housing that is flexible to changing household size.

The concept of layers of construction with different life expectancies and levels of embodied energy leads to an architectural treatment that favours thickness of construction in the permanent parts, and thinness elsewhere. The perimeter walls for instance should be thick and super-insulated, and research suggests the house roof should be so too. Thick external elements provide good structural robustness, a high level of air and water tightness, and adequate space for insulation between leaves of construction. Thick walls also lead to good aesthetics and

1.13 *Changing relationship between heating, passive gains and insulation in the 20th century house. Brian Edwards/BRE*

1.14 *Preferred material choices in terms of embodied energy.*

1.15 *The importance of the house in creating sustainable communities.*

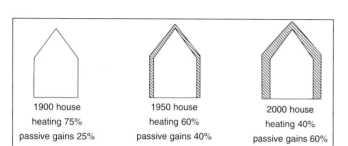

1900 house
heating 75%
passive gains 25%

1950 house
heating 60%
passive gains 40%

2000 house
heating 40%
passive gains 60%

a feeling of security so essential in housing. The sub division of space and service runs should be independent of walls, providing flexibility and upgradeability.

Buildability is a key aspect of sustainable housing and is linked to the question of embodied energy. In order to reduce costs and bring low energy design within the reach of first time buyers, it is important that complexity is avoided. Housing design needs to be simple in concept using readily understood drawings so that the contractor can build it well and efficiently. The low energy house will be more expensive to construct than the standard Building Regulations house but it should not be more difficult to understand. The extra costs of an eco-house vary according to design and specification but are usually 5–15% greater than the norm (the Oxford Solar House by Susan Roaf (Figure 4.1) cost 11% above the average for comparable dwellings). As a general rule, the super-insulated house incorporating a range of low energy measures costs about £70/m² above the average, adding about 8% to construction costs with a payback period of about six to ten years (at 1999 prices).

A well designed house today constructed to just above Building Regulations standards has energy bills slightly greater for hot water as against space heating. This is the first time in UK housing that water heating exceeds the cost of keeping the internal fabric warm. The 1930s house spent 25% on water heating and 75% on space heating but the house of the future may well reverse these figures, especially if renewable energy sources are employed. As energy in use figures fall, the embodied energy cost rises in importance. Usually embodied energy (i.e. the energy used to make, transport and employ the building material) is about 10–20% of the total energy in use over 50 years.

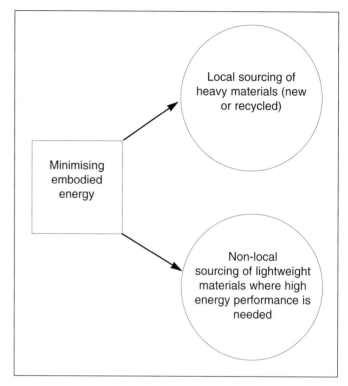

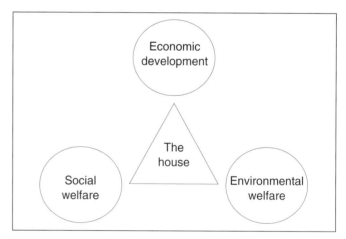

However, with super-insulated houses the figure can approach 18–20%. A simple rule to follow with embodied energy is to avoid bringing heavy materials from further than 30 km away and to use imported lightweight materials where there are technical advantages (e.g. low energy, high performance Swedish windows) from further afield.

1.16 *Ecolonia, a model of sustainable housing from Holland masterplanned by Lucien Kroll.*

Flexibility and employment

Social sustainability in housing requires adaptability of the structure. House types need to change in order to avoid the need for families to move. Sustainable communities are lasting communities where families invest long periods of time in their neighbourhood. Sustainable housing depends upon it being valued by tenants or owners. The roots to this reside in perceptions of health, comfort, flexibility of use and enhanced asset value. Housing is not sustainable if it is cold, damp, unhealthy, expensive to run and deteriorating in financial value. Neither is the community sustainable if there is fear of crime, if employment is not available or if the schools and health clinics provide a poor service.

Although a house is a home, it is also the main building block of successful communities. The home as a family unit addresses three distinct policy territories – economic development, social welfare and environmental welfare. The more the interactions are explored, the greater the success of the housing enterprise. For example, if local developers, designers and construction workers are employed, the more likely the success of the undertaking. Local skills and knowledge mean that local suppliers are more likely to be used, with the result that the development will be seen as 'belonging' and the money involved will be retained in the community. This is true of initiatives such as combined heat and power schemes (CHP) that exploit their waste energy to heat local homes and industries. Also bearing in mind fuel poverty and the poor energy performance of many housing estates, CHP is better used to heat existing properties than new estates.

Housing construction is not only a question of providing new homes but also of creating jobs in the process. The trend towards industrialisation of the UK construction

The green context

1.17 *Plan and section of steel framed housing for the Peabody Trust in London by architects Cartwright Pickard.*

8000

metal roofing system

lightweight steel walkways

terracotta rainscreen cladding

perforated aluminium sheet balustrade

lightweight steel cross bracing

76mm dia. steel columns

130mm dia. steel columns

300mm high pre-cast plinth

Typical section through accommodation

1.18 *Environmental factors as the basis for job creation and innovative housing design.*

1.19 *Existing buildings should be the target of any national energy strategy.*

industry stimulated by the Latham and Egan reports means a reduction in the number of construction workers employed. This can be offset by linking job creation to eco-renovation on the housing site. If there are no jobs generated by a housing development, there tends to be little interest amongst local decision makers. The answer lies in exploiting the advantages of industrialised production in the provision of buildings, whilst creating jobs in the one-off aspects of site development, such as land renewal, ecological repair, energy efficiency measures and local power generation. This results in cost effective housing and by exploiting energy efficiency and environmental upgrading, in the provision also of new jobs and training programmes of relevance to the future. In fact, the larger the overlap of the energy, ecology and environmental aspects of housing development, the greater the number of jobs likely to be generated per housing unit. It is important that ecological imperatives become both the driving force in innovative design and in job creation.

The importance of the existing housing stock

In the UK the rate of redevelopment of the housing stock is under 1% per year. Although society faces the prospect of constructing 4.1 million new households by 2016 in order to cater for the anticipated growth in small households, the balance of sustainability benefits lies in concentrating upon upgrading the existing stock of some 20 million houses. Research later in the book suggests that on energy grounds alone, we should in Britain be replacing the existing stock by

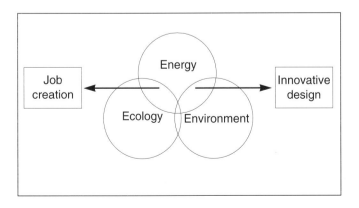

2% per year, though resource limitation may prohibit this. Much of the poorer end of the housing stock (mostly built in the 1960s) does not lend itself to cost effective energy upgrading at current levels of grant and energy price. But for the majority of houses in Britain, energy performance can be enhanced with a payback period of five to eight years. Some measures are tried and tested, they include: double or triple glazing; improved ventilation control; higher insulation levels; and improvement to boiler efficiency. Since the utility suppliers have a duty under the energy acts to conserve energy as well as sell it, there is some argument for the gas and electricity supply companies taking over energy management in the home. This could lead to free energy surveys for each householder in the UK, advice (and grants) on upgrading measures with the utility supplier taking over the quality control of any subsequent work. The benefit to the customer would be lower energy bills, for the supply company an enhanced image, and for the government lower national CO_2 emission levels.

1.20 *The importance of housing to social and environmental harmony.*

1.21 *Key policy interdependencies revolving around housing.*

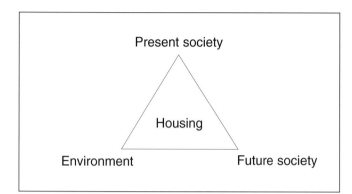

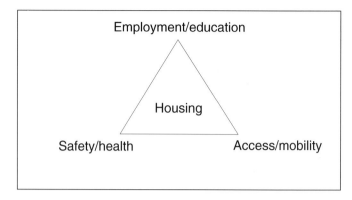

The case for greater attention being directed to existing dwellings is now well established. It is estimated that the cost of energy retrofitting the existing stock of housing in the UK to 1990 Building Regulations standards is about £35 billion. This would produce an annual national energy saving of nearly £2.5 billion, giving a payback period of about 15 years.[1] Such action would reduce the amount of CO_2 released into the atmosphere from about 560 million tonnes per year to under 400 million tonnes. If energy costs increased in real terms (via an energy or environment tax) the payback period would reduce depending upon the level of fuel tax. The argument is overwhelmingly in favour of a national campaign in favour of energy upgrading of existing dwellings. There are the obvious savings to be made in CO_2 emissions (allowing the UK to meet its international obligation), in the reduction of fuel poverty, in lower prevalence of building related illness (asthma, bronchitis etc.), in enhanced comfort, and in the retrofitting needed to job creation. For the government, re-skilling of the workforce via domestic energy action (perhaps undertaken on behalf of the energy supplier) could have advantages as great as that of CO_2 reduction. Certainly, the jobs generated would be in areas where unemployment is high (older housing estates, depressed former mining villages) and hence addressing the crucial social dimension to sustainable development.

The social dimension

In spite of the necessary concentration upon energy usage because of global warming, sustainable housing is a broad and complex field. The concept of sustainable development embraces a compact between society today, environmental resources and society's future needs. Put simply there is a triangular structure of interdependencies at a strategic or global level with housing at the centre. The Rio conference on the environment (1992), the Habitat Convention in Constantinople (1996) and the Kyoto conference on global warming (1997) are all landmark agreements impacting upon housing.

In order to shape action in support of sustainable housing, it is necessary to distinguish between social issues and environmental ones. For example, social sustainability requires that communities have access to employment, to healthy and safe environments, and mobility. Hence, a triangle exists here of interdependencies between employment/education and safety/health and access/mobility, each revolving around the issue of housing.

It is easy to see how unsustainable much existing housing has become when set alongside these priorities. Many housing estates suffer from poor employment prospects, under-performing schools, the home environment is not safe, healthy or comfortable and transport is too poor or

1.22 *Key interactions with building design – energy, environment and ecology.*

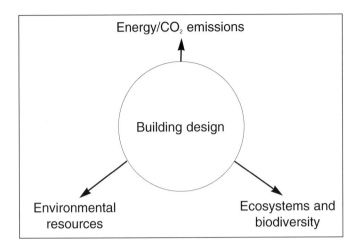

Energy/CO$_2$ emissions

Building design

Environmental resources

Ecosystems and biodiversity

Table 1.7 Housing estate sustainability indicators

Topic	Indicator
Energy	CO$_2$ per house type per year
Environmental resources	Water usage per house type per year
Ecosystem	Blackbird population per year

expensive (Easterhouse, near Glasgow is a good example). As a result many people suffer from social exclusion.

Sustainable housing has to grasp the nettle of social provision, equity and justice. Every line a town planner or architect draws is in a sense a political act. The line of exclusion is indelibly drawn across the face of Britain, often in the pretext of land use zoning, density control or transportation planning. Sustainability has to break down the injustices inherent in our binary systems – social versus private housing, greenfield versus brownfield land, employment versus welfare, car versus public transport. Sustainable housing provides the mechanism to create integrated balanced communities where there was once division by class, race or opportunity.

Integration of the three E's – energy, ecology and environment

Architects and developers have little direct say upon social provision but they need to be aware of the divisions that they perpetrate or help break down. Where they can, however, have influence is in another triangular set of relationships. The various international agreements on the environment and climate change mean that building design has three distinct perspectives to consider – energy, ecology and environment.

The concentration upon low energy design is no longer sufficient if true sustainability is to be met, but conversely, sustainable development that does not have at its centre an energy strategy is also invalid. Designers now need to incorporate into masterplans the regenerative potential of ecosystems and to consider in a holistic fashion the environmental resource implications (from water to rainforests) of their development decisions. It is a tall order, especially with inadequate information on lifecycle impacts and a construction industry that appears reluctant to innovate in the housing sector. But it is possible to extract indicators from the complex picture and use these to highlight good practice at a local level. For example, with energy, one could relatively easily model different housing designs against CO$_2$ emissions per year (using BRE templates); with environmental resources, one could measure water use; and with ecosystems, one could use a single species (such as the blackbird or toad) as an indicator of local biodiversity. By using indicators to model or monitor performance, the full complexity of sustainable development could be reduced to measurable parts. It will not tell you the whole picture, but as a design or management tool it could point in the right direction.

1.23 *Details matter in sustainable housing: (a) dustbin and compost store; (b) trellis for growing plants; (c) sheltered entrance.*

(a)   *(b)*   *(c)*

Principles of sustainable housing design

Although there is still some disagreement regarding detail, most architects and developers acknowledge that sustainable housing neighbourhoods will need to display the following general features:

- high density, mixed use and diversified tenure
- integration of land use and transport planning with emphasis upon public means of transportation
- urban layout that creates shelter and safety
- the exploitation of renewable energy supplies (wind, sun, etc.)
- capture of rainfall for certain water uses
- use of open space (streets, parks and squares) to facilitate social interaction and ecological wellbeing
- pollution and waste strategies
- creation of natural habitats integrated with housing.

At the individual building level, sustainable housing will probably display a further list of features:

- healthy, comfortable, secure homes
- householder able to adapt or extend space
- designed-in ability to upgrade
- low energy design exploiting renewable energy sources
- super-insulated homes
- low water consumption.

In addition, there may be other characteristics sought by particular tenant groups or owner occupiers. These include:

- disabled access (no steps)
- use of 'smart technologies' to enhance security
- spiritual design (nature, feng shui)
- ability to work from home.

Sustainable housing (as against sustainable houses) will take on quite a different form when under the influence of these features, compared with much of the housing built in the past 100 years. As such, the imperatives of sustainability will lead to a new housing aesthetic with consequences for how planning authorities conduct their con-

1.24 *The re-interpretation of housing traditions is key to sustainability.*
Architect: McGurn, Logan, Duncan and Opfer

trolling function, how developers appeal to the taste of consumers, and how architects approach the design of housing.

New design solutions

The scale of new urban housing required provides an opportunity to innovate. The twin forces of growth in provision coupled with the sustainability agenda offer a chance to explore 'newness' after a long period of neglect of housing design. Of the 4.1 million homes required by the second decade of the next century, it is predicted that 3.5 million will be for first time buyers. These are mainly single people for whom life in the suburbs will be unsuitable. Familiar with European patterns of living, conscious of the excitement and opportunities offered by cities, the first time single buyer is more likely to embrace new design approaches than traditional family units. This is why sustainable housing offers unprecedented opportunity to explore both the creativity of city life and modes of living that place the environment under reduced stress.

This requires a reinterpretation of the typology of housing, from the semi-detached house to the urban terrace and city street. The family of the future is likely to be based upon single parents, non-nuclear units, childless couples and extended inter-generational groups. The 'third age' family does not necessarily require a semi or a bungalow, nor does the working single person. For all these groups new forms are needed, new relationships of the home to the street and the urban block. Standardised production by traditional housing providers will increasingly be replaced by architects who can meet the particular demands of specific communities.

To implement sustainable housing two distinct strategies are needed. First, a campaign of persuasion and demonstration projects to show that the new demands can be met in an attractive fashion. The UK is well behind The Netherlands, Germany and Denmark in the range of sustainable communities actually built – education through demonstration is the key to change.

Second, there will need to be greater regulation of the housing market by stricter planning controls, tougher performance standards for new houses, and higher

1.25 *Design holds the key to broadening the appeal of sustainability.*
Architect: Jeremy Dixon, LDDC

1.26 *Old and new housing, high and medium density – these are the mixtures sustainability seeks to establish. St Saviour's Dock in London Docklands.*
Architect: Michael Squire and Partners

upgrading levels for the existing stock. Such measures are needed not just in the energy field but in water use, environmental and waste management, in transport policy, and in action to create local biodiversity in housing areas. To date the emphasis has been upon energy enhancement, not comprehensive environmental upgrading or the development of physical measures to help build communities in a sustainable social sense. Change in government outlook is required, but so too are changes in professional practice, in the housing development process, in fiscal policy and in lifestyle. All of us are involved in bringing about the new age of sustainability.

The problem with meeting future targets for CO_2 reduction is not lack of improvement in the performance

1.27 *Good design can help package dense forms of urban living. Compass Point in East London.*
Architect: Jeremy Dixon, LDDC

of new buildings, but the sheer scale of new accommodation required. Saving on the existing stock is overwhelmed by the anticipated growth in households. The 4.1 million new homes required by 2016 (3.1 million of which will be for people living alone) makes the meeting of UK and EU targets difficult. Not only is the number of new houses almost unprecedented but expectations of lifestyle are rising. This puts pressure on energy, water and other resources often in unexpected ways. For example, the drive for healthy living means an increase in fresh imported foods. Research in the USA has shown that every glass of orange juice consumed requires two glasses of oil to get it to the breakfast table. Rising standards of living worldwide coupled with an increasing population results ulti-

mately in ever more CO_2 released to the atmosphere. In the UK, total carbon dioxide emissions now exceed 560 million tonnes, or more than 10 tonnes per person per year.

The emphasis upon dense and compact forms of living, which is the main design advice to date for sustainable housing, carries inevitably problems for social behaviour and human interaction. Antisocial tenants can undermine the creation of sustainable communities but conversely people will need to accept less privacy and less silence as sustainable housing takes hold. Society will need to accept a 'forgiveness factor' in order for the change to high density, mixed land-use lifestyles to occur. The old separation of living, working, education and leisure will end and in its

1.28 *Having fun with urban housing. Plan of Cascades on the Isle of Dogs, London by CZWG.*

1.29 *Nature can be brought indoors to enhance spiritual and physical well-being. Brian Edwards' house, Causewayend, Scotland.*

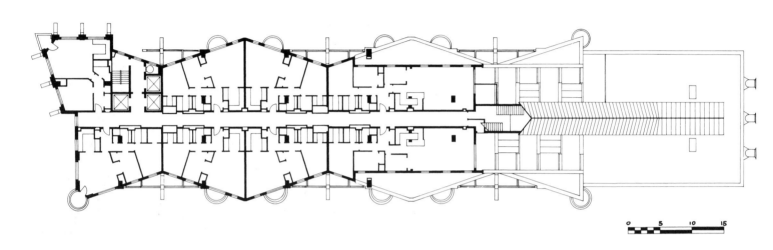

place we will have dense overlapping communities of people, lifestyles and urban activities. The main mechanism to make this bearable for the bulk of people is the power of design. The new sustainable communities will be designled, not developer- or council-led. Good urban, landscape and building design will make the difference between successful, sustainable communities and socially rejected, unsustainable ones. Sustainability provides a great opportunity for the architectural professional to become involved again in the provision of homes on a national scale. In fact, DETR projections show that over 2 million homes are likely to be built between 2000 and 2010 (a rate of 200,000 per year).

Reference

1. *Reducing the Greenhouse Effect by Domestic Insulation*, Eurisol - UK Mineral Wool Association, St Albans, 1989.

1.30 *Key relationships in sustainable housing (top left).*

1.31 *Compact development of mixed use – housing, shops, offices – in London (bottom left).*
Architect: Julyan Wickham

1.32 *Compact development of mixed use – housing, studios and shops – in Glasgow.*
Architect: Elder and Cannon

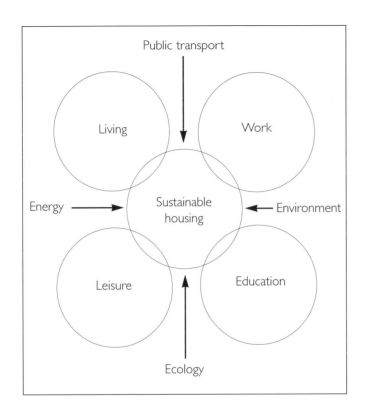

Housing and transport

DAVID LOCK

Over the past two years, there have been significant changes in the government outlook on planning, especially the relationship between urban development and transport. Planning policy guidance has moved towards ensuring that new development is located in areas well served by non-car modes. Planning Policy Guidance (PPG) 13 on *Transport* seeks to reduce journeys made by car by proposing integrated transport solutions made possible by enhanced development densities and mixed land-uses. Since existing urban areas are better served by public transport than land outside cities, the effect is to direct development towards brownfield, as against greenfield sites (especially in the green belt).

Planning policy guidance has signalled a change in outlook at the centre of government. Local authorities are now given a clear policy framework on how CO_2 emissions can be reduced by effective action through the planning system. PPG 13, plus PPG 6: *Town Centres and Retailing*, and PPG 1 *General Politics and Principles* reinforce the message that housing densities need to rise, that only sites served by public transport (or capable of being served) will receive planning consent; that regional planning and transportation infrastructure need to be integrated; that mixed use and diversified tenure are the preferred model for new development and that enhanced development densities should be sought around transport nodes.

The new commitment to integrating land use planning and transport has major ramifications for housing. In fact, one could say that housing is not sustainable unless it can be served by non-car modes, at least in the medium to long term. Current thinking and demonstration projects (such as the Millennium Village at Greenwich) based upon

2.1 *The model for sustainable housing exists in many older towns. Here in Leamington Spa medium density town housing encloses a semi-public garden. Cars are segregated between access and through routes with priority given to the pedestrian at the building edge.*

2.2 *Steps, railings and canopy all signal the controlled transition between the public and private realm.*

high density, mixed use neighbourhoods closely integrated with various transport modes (walking, cycling, bus, tram, light rail, suburban rail, intercity rail) are increasingly the model for major urban regeneration projects, for the development of town expansion schemes and new settlements in the countryside.

Sustainable housing is only achieved if designers and developers join up issues usually considered in a compartmentalised fashion. Housing type, tenure mix and density need to be considered alongside movement and transportation. Social well-being, environmental responsibility and design excellence need also to be put into the same equation. It is easy to solve problems in isolation but sustainable housing requires a high level of connectivity of thought and process.

The green context

2.3 *The traditional high density urban block reconsidered at Swedish Quays in London Docklands by architects Price and Cullen.*

Housing probably has a greater impact upon global and social harmony than any other building type. Housing needs to support family life, community cohesion and ecological well-being. To achieve true sustainability we need to think about housing design, about how we live and move, about the environmental consequences of different choices available. Transport is a useful indicator of connected thinking and by using CO_2 emission levels we can begin to equate design choices with impacts. For instance, modelling CO_2 levels allows the characteristics of estate location, layout, density and house type to highlight the integrated nature of building energy costs and those resulting from different transport choices. Just as in the home where energy is a useful indicator of sustainable design, one can use energy to illuminate the bigger urban picture. Too

often in the past, the BRE and others have highlighted energy within the building, without looking at the broader consequences for the urban transport system. Given that 29% of UK CO_2 emissions are the result of transportation (mostly private car-based), the lack of integration across the field of urban design has left us with a legacy of problems from the past 15 years.

It is remarkable how quickly a consensus has emerged since the Kyoto conference on climate change in 1997. Government, local authorities, developers and the professions generally now share the same vision, or at least accept the same broad principles. There are still dissenting voices from, for instance, the National House Builders Federation, but from John Prescott, the Deputy Prime Minister downwards, there is agreement that sustainable housing will be based upon a combination of:

- compact, medium to high density forms (but not high rise)
- mix of land uses based upon overlapping zones of living, working, leisure and shopping
- public transport orientated urban design
- pedestrian friendly streets
- well defined public spaces
- integration of development and nature on site
- development patterns dictated by walking or cycle distances.

Although the 'new urbanism' movement, which the above list encapsulates, is essentially the rediscovery of the traditional city, it has been brought into focus by American urban theorists such as Peter Calthorpe in his important book *The Next American Metropolis*. But what is pertinent about the new urbanism is the coalition between civilised values for urban living and sustainable design. For just as Lord Rogers argues in the Urban Task Force prospectus, 'we must ... promote more compact urban environments ... discourage greenfield development ... and create more vital urban communities'.[1] Vitality is a product of interaction of people in a convivial, dynamic environment. Cities are, unlike sprawling amorphous suburbs, centres of creativity and innovation.

The new urbanism has at its core the principle that public transport should determine the location, size, organisation and density of neighbourhoods. Movement and connectivity underpin all the development and design decisions - it is the basis for the spatial, social and aesthetic order. By giving priority to public transport (or transit as the Americans call it), the planning of new or revitalised older neighbourhoods takes on an immediate web of sociability and reduced ecological impact.

If public transport provision is at the centre of sustainable neighbourhoods, the railway station is clearly the hub of a system that includes also buses, taxis, trams, cycles and movement on foot. Cars have their place but their penetration and physical presence should be limited. Since the different transportation modes have their own dimensional efficiency, there are preferred configurations for neighbourhood centre, sub-centres and distances between the core and perimeter. Usually, the transport oriented sustainable community has a limit of around 400m (5 minutes walk) between the home and nearest service centre where shops, bus stop or train station may be located. In simple townships this means that the distance between sub-nodes is about 800m or 1,750 feet (2,000 feet makes a good rule of thumb). Light rail or tram stops are therefore spaced every 800 m or so, bus stops every 400m and main transport connections (via the railway station) every 6–8km. The pattern is rather more linear than concentric because of the dictates of the railway line, but at each station concentric rings radiate outwards to the limit of about 800m.

Around the station density of development increases and so does the integration of different land uses. The integration is in both plan and section with a useful further guiding rule that land uses should be symmetrical across the street (shops facing shops, etc.) but asymmetrical across the urban block. Asymmetry within the block provides for the close integration of different urban functions, and helps maintain densities so that the majority of movements can be on foot, bicycle or by public transport. The pattern also suggests a gradual reduction in density from the centre outwards – a development gradation from say 60 dwellings per hectare in the central areas to 40 at the edge.

Well structured settlements will be a feature of sustainable communities. The countryside will be accessible, open space within towns will be well formed and cared for, streets will have space for nature and play as well as movement, and there will be a clearly defined urban centre where civic and major commercial activities are located. In this sense, urban design and sustainable development are essential partners.

The model for the sustainable community is partly the Garden City Movement, partly also the planned townships of 18th century America (such as Williamsburg) and partly our own early new towns in the UK (such as Letchworth). Planning and landscape design are essential components but unlike earlier examples, density of occupation and compaction of built form are vital ingredients. Densities will generally be significantly higher than in past

2.4 *Crisis of car dominated urbanism. Sustainable housing needs to give public space back to people.*

2.5 *Example of the new urbanism by the River Clyde in Glasgow designed by David Lick Associates (DLA).*

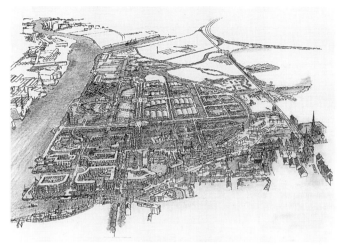

model communities, except perhaps for New Lanark in Scotland (built in 1790) which provides an excellent example of compact, medium density, mixed use development.

The pattern described is both a recipe for new settlements and for the regeneration of former industrial sites in existing towns. It is important that the economic and legislative framework adjusts quickly to the new priorities brought about by our interest in sustainability. One of the constraints to implementing change is the reluctance of planning authorities to grant planning permission for development that exceeds specified densities, provides limited or no parking space for private cars, and puts land uses together in novel fashions. Sustainable development is a concept that challenges most professional practice, particularly the way the development industry parcels decisions into tidy boxes.

If public transport promises to provide the spatial order of sustainable communities then town expansion schemes or new settlements (of up to 25,000 people) need to develop around multi-modal interchanges. In the old days these were called railway stations, but to be effective in moving people the railway needs to interact with other forms of movement. This entails requiring developers to help pay for station construction and to design their projects so that connection to stations is made easy. To facilitate this, planning densities and land uses could inten-

sify around stations thereby linking capital investment with income generation. The greater the compaction of development, the lower the likely subsidy from public bodies.

Since railway lines tend to be noisy it is important that a buffer zone is created along rail-based transport corridors. This could consist of a tree lined boulevard if trams were involved and perhaps a wildlife corridor 50m wide on either side of the railway line. Such corridors readily convert into green wedges which act as grids of biodiversity as well as providing routes for cycleways or walking.

Accessibility is a key factor in the success of places – communities that are not readily accessible inside their boundaries and out are hardly sustainable. Access is about safe, secure and healthy means of movement for all – families, children, elderly, rich and poor. Too often today access is limited to those with cars with the result that some communities are deprived of good quality services. One of the key performance criteria for sustainable communities is that of accessibility at macro and micro levels.

Since streets are the main movement corridors of sustainable housing, there needs to be provision for a variety of transport modes close to houses. Car access is at present needed but government policy in the UK is to limit journeys made by car and to encourage households to survive with one, not two or three cars. The street is also

2.6 *The electric car of the future in the Disney town of Celebration in Florida.*

2.7 *Ebbsfleet masterplan in Kent. Spatial clarity, high density and ecology combined. Architects: DLA*

the corridor for movement on foot and by bicycle. To encourage such transport (and movement on foot is a form of transport) pavements need to be wide, safe and free of obstacles. Too often in cities pavement space for pedestrians is obstructed by traffic signs, litter bins, transport barriers, bus shelters and utility poles. Sustainable neighbourhoods will have wide pavements (room for two or three people to walk and talk together), perhaps a protective barrier of trees between cars and people and a separate marked cycleway all created within current street dimensions (by restricting cars to one narrow lane). Streets and squares will also be overlooked by windows and some street corners may have community shops. It will add up to a safer, cleaner, less polluting and more

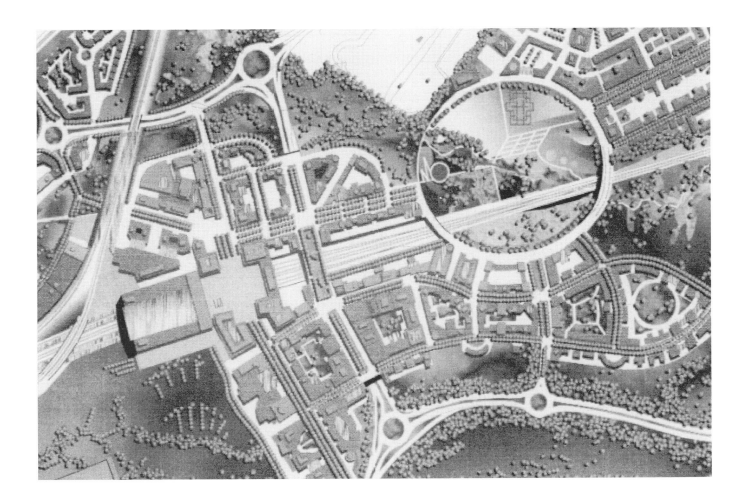

The green context

2.8 *Masterplan for redevelopment of disused airfield in Ipswich, Suffolk.*
Architects: DLA

2.9 *Abstract model of a public transport orientated development.*
Architects: DLA

2.10 *Artist's view of new urban streetscape based upon integrated transport.*
Architects: DLA

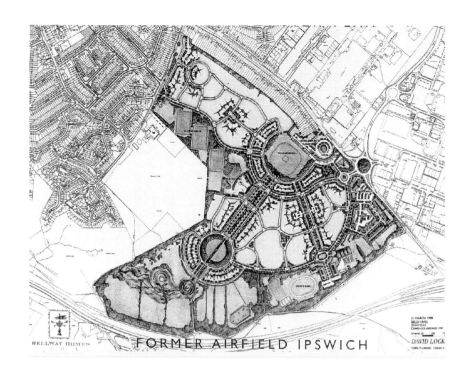

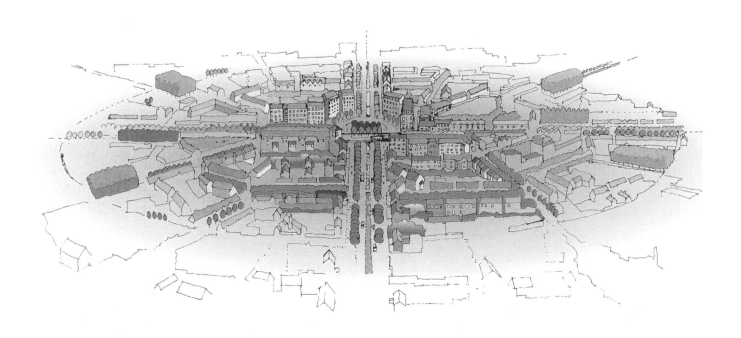

tranquil form of urban life which may help address the current decline in the quality of English cities and the preference for suburban as against urban lifestyles.

The model of sustainable housing outlined is only viable on developments of around 40 houses per hectare. Densities below this do not support public transport and the close integration of other activities such as shops. However, the average density of development on greenfield land in the UK is currently 22 houses per hectare and 28 houses per hectare on brownfield sites.[2] Hence the need for stricter density controls and the creation of new model communities in the inner city such as the regeneration of the Gorbals area of Glasgow where 64 houses per hectare have been built. Here the masterplan of 1990 by CZWG architects established well defined streets and parks with tree lined boulevards along which buses connect with underground and suburban rail services. The buildings are mainly three storey terraced houses and four storey flats some of which support shops on the ground floor and incorporate offices above. Generous private sector subsidies were involved, and the Scots culture of apartment living helped. Attempts at direct reproduction in England have begun in Manchester, Leeds and London.

High quality urban design is, according to Richard Caborn the Planning Minister, a 'specific requirement for sustainable development'.[3] The linking of good urban design with transport planning and sustainable housing is the theme of two recent proposals illustrated below. The first is the new community at Clyst Hayes near Exeter which utilises an existing railway station to develop a high density sustainable township located near Exeter Airport. It takes advantage of poorly developed existing infrastructure (i.e. the station) to create a small new town of about 8,000 people based upon the 'walkable neighbourhood principle'.

Another much larger project at Ebbsfleet in north Kent takes advantage of former cement quarries alongside a proposed Channel Tunnel railway station (Figure 2.7). Here the scheme, which received outline planning permission in 1998, is based upon mixed use, high density living with intensification of activities around the station. The Ebbsfleet mode is part of a new metropolitan scheme that will contain 30,000 homes built by a number of developers working to design briefs that have sustainability at their centre. Ebbsfleet will contain 8.5 million square feet of mixed office, leisure and retail accommodation, some of which will be constructed in blocks also containing housing.

The form of Ebbsfleet is based upon compaction with clearly defined centres, edges, parks and linking streets. At present in the UK only 20% of journeys over 1km are made by non-car modes, but at Ebbsfleet the transport system is designed on the expectation that, through the integration of development and transportation, 40% can be achieved. Connectivity is the key to the masterplan: planning, building design, managing the development process and partnership funding between developers and transport providers will together create a model sustainable community alongside the Thames. The intention is to target not just energy but water conservation by working with Blue Circle Cement, who have been quarrying the land, to experiment with new ways of collecting, recycling and purifying water rising from the aquifer on site.

Both the Clyst Hayes and Ebbsfleet projects show that sustainable communities can be created in the UK. The new urbanism movement provides useful lessons or paradigms of urban design that are applicable on both sides of the Atlantic. Integrating development with public transportation provides the justification for raising development densities, thereby improving the social mix and sense of liveability. If urban design benefits from the process, so too do the economics of development. As densities rise around the inter-modal interchange, the prospect of profits increase and with it the chance to turn theory into practice.

References

1. *Urban Task Force* prospectus, Department of the Environment, Transport and the Regions, July 1998, p. 9.
2. 'Government Urges Density Standards' *Planning*, 30 October 1998, p. 1.
3. Ibid.

3

Building and landscape

ANDREW GRANT

Global economic systems pay scant regard to the environment. Landscape quality and environmental capacity are rarely part of the development equation at a macro or micro level. As a consequence global ecology is seen as a luxury and landscape design, at the level of housing estates, is often treated as a marketing cosmetic.

The human landscape and natural landscape are inescapably entwined. Action we take has consequences at various levels, though society is not always aware of the full impact at the local, regional, national and international scale. Decisions made by architects and engineers have enormous ramifications upon biodiversity, habitats and species survival. Deputy Prime Minister John Prescott's recent announcement that quality of life indicators in the UK will in future include bird populations, should effectively curb modern agricultural practice with its emphasis upon the exploitation of CAP grants coupled with the ruthless application of crop monocultures.

The World Wide Fund for Nature reported in 1998 that the planet has lost a third of its global natural world in the past 20 years. Or put another way, in less than a generation we have destroyed a third of all virgin habitats in the world. Such destruction is usually the result of gaining materials for the construction industry – timber, aggregates – or the result of drainage schemes or forest destruction to facilitate agricultural or physical development. As a consequence, planet Earth loses around 20,000 species per year, most of which we have barely learnt to understand in terms of their systemic role or their potential for the development of new crops or medicines. Extinction is for ever – no genetic cloning will bring back lost biodiversity. In spite of the agreement reached by 170 nations at the Earth Summit at Rio in 1992 to preserve global biodiver-

3.1 *Human and natural landscapes need to integrate through the medium of cities. Architect: LDDC*

Table 3.1 Goal and principles of UK Action Plan on Biodiversity

Overall goal
To conserve and enhance biological diversity within the UK and to contribute to the conservation of global biodiversity through all appropriate mechanisms

Underlying principles
— where biological resources are used, such use should be sustainable
— wise use should be ensured for non-renewable resources
— the conservation of biodiversity requires the care and involvement of individuals and communities as well as governmental processes
— conservation of biodiversity should be an integral part of government programmes, policy and action
— conservation practice and policy should be based upon a sound knowledge base
— the precautionary principle should guide decisions

Source: UK government report UK Action Plan for Biodiversity, HMSO, 1994

3.2 *Cities are models of consumption – energy, land, minerals, water and space.*

sity, society seems unaware of the connection between physical development, habitats and species.

Part of the loss of the natural world is caused by the accelerating rate of consumption. Today in the West we consume three times more food than we need to stay fit and healthy. The UK also produces three times the carbon dioxide per person compared to the world average. Growth is not in itself a problem, but how we grow and consume is. For example, the 4.1 million new households required in Britain by 2016 could destroy, according to the Council for the Preservation of Rural England (CPRE), 500 square miles of open countryside. Alternatively, it could lead to the regeneration of the same area of contaminated brownfield land.

To shift development to brownfield sites as the RIBA and others advocate requires new tools, mechanisms and design approaches. Conventional wisdom and well established practices do not always hold true for the age of sustainability. For instance, society needs to discover the benefits of urban living, to establish new ways of bringing nature into cities, and to exploit the regenerational effect of landscape upon the health of soils and the spirit of people.

Landscape is at the core of bringing a wider understanding of environmental capacity. Landscape design can help educate people about the complex dependencies present in the environment. Design, whether architectural, urban or landscape, engages in complicated interactions between energy, ecology and development ethics. For example, in its strategic approach to land utilisation, development could begin to demonstrate, at least symbolically, that the population of London requires the whole productive area of the UK to produce the food to sustain the capital. This requires a different approach to landscape design than the one that is usually employed, one where gardens and allotments figure as both productive and educational elements.

The designs of ancient settlements contain lessons that are relevant today. Learning from the vernacular entails valuing the process rather than the product; a process that is usually fashioned by ecological awareness – climate, social patterns, craft skills, locally sourced materials, impact upon fauna and flora, etc. Vernacular buildings or places are usually long lived because they are physically, ecologically and socially robust. Sustainability is the pathway to rediscovering the worth of vernacular solutions, and in learning to value community based processes rather than those that are development led.

We can learn from both the Bronze Age settlement of Skara Brae in the Orkneys and the Roman townships of Britain. In both cases buildings and landscape modification were integrated to create shelter, to produce food and to form space for community interactions. The Romans introduced water as an amenity to Britain; their settlements exploited layout to achieve the maximum of solar gain and gridded streets were provided as service corridors and circulation routes. At Skara Brae local materials in the form of stone slabs and turf were turned into doors, walls, roof and furniture. Without timber these early Orkney settlers improvised and worked with nature, not against it.

3.3 *The Earth Centre, near Doncaster masterplanned by Grant Associates. There is a clear ecological concept in the regeneration of this large brownfield site in Yorkshire.*

3.4 *These new houses at Findhorn in Scotland have much to teach about the relationship between building and landscape. Notice the communal bicycle shed in foreground.*

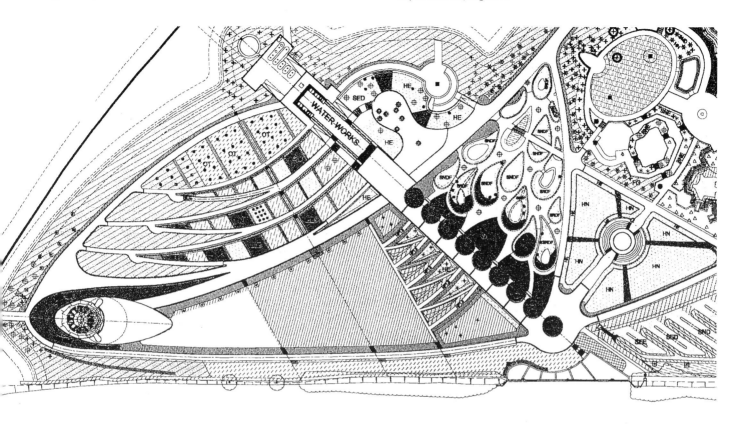

More recently, the urban vernacular of terraced housing provides helpful lessons, especially that created in 18th century Britain. Bath, Edinburgh and New Lanark have excellent examples of how buildings and landscape can be combined. At Bath's Royal Crescent the layout is in effect a sun scoop with the curving terrace embracing a garden and view to the south. With the need for greater shelter the terraces of Edinburgh enclose communal gardens which are set as green rectangles within the urban mass. In both cases houses and flats share the terraces with shops, offices and workspace beneath. Land use integration in compact urban form is not new to Britain. At New Lanark a different kind of synthesis of built form is achieved around the imperatives of working harmony, social progress and respect for unmanicured nature.

Early in the 19th century Nash, with his so called 'jerry built' houses, also created useful prototypes of sustainable housing. They were cement rendered and painted,

3.5 *New Lanark: a model of social harmony and sustainability.*

3.6 *The European model of sustainable urbanism from Palma – compact forms with people friendly streets and tree planted avenues.*

3.5 *New Lanark: a model of social harmony and sustainability.*

3.6 *The European model of sustainable urbanism from Palma – compact forms with people friendly streets and tree planted avenues.*

organised into handsome terraces, built around parks and squares, and created good living conditions for all social classes. Haussmann in Paris, a couple of decades later, achieved another excellent model of compact urbanism with integrated public health services and a respect for nature which was brought into contact with peoples' lives via treelined boulevards. These and many others are lessons we can use today, but the process of development must be understood as well as the form.

Proximity to nature has many benefits for communities – health, social well-being, tranquillity and visual amenity. In fact, the view of a tree or being able to hear birdsong is a good indicator of sustainability. At the new Bibliothèque Nationale de Paris, the centre of the library is a garden of semi-mature closely planted Scots pines. The contrast with the harsh architectural forms is uplifting, a useful reminder when reflecting upon the wisdom of books that nature itself provides another philosophical support for life.

Architects tend to use energy as the guiding light of sustainable design. Energy as such has little benefit to the landscape designer where other resources are more useful guides to good practice. Increasingly water is employed to provide insight into landscape design decisions. Water is central to life and hence is a useful indication of good practice in terms of sustainable landscape design. Water also provides qualitative and quantitative measures which can give information on ecological processes. The recycling of water on site, the capture of rainfall for certain domestic purposes, the treatment of waste water through reedbeds are all decisions that flow from using water not energy as an indicator of good sustainable practice.

Technical matters require of the landscape designer a good grasp of science and a sound basis on which to exercise judgement. Ecology provides the ethical parameters for decision making. Without good science we are lost, but equally, without sound judgement we will have no basis upon which to forge a sustainable future. Nature as a paradigm combines both in an elegant fashion.

3.7 *Housing and water in physical partnership in Surrey Docks, London. Masterplan: Conran Roche*

4

Renewable energy in housing

DEREK TAYLOR

Renewable energy

Renewable energy can be used to provide electricity, mechanical power, heat or fuel, certain renewable energy technologies are the fastest growing global energy sources, currently expanding at growth rates not seen since the early days of microcomputers. The UK has perhaps the widest choice of renewable energy sources of any country in the world. There is wind energy, water power, solar energy, biofuels, geothermal energy, tidal and wave energy.

Renewable energy can be used in buildings in one or more of the following ways:

- it can be extracted elsewhere and delivered via the conventional delivery channels and networks
- it can be extracted locally and used locally
- it can be extracted at the site of the building(s)
- it can be extracted at the building or by the building envelope.

Solar energy

Solar energy has been used to provide useful energy for centuries, principally as a source of heat and light.

Using solar energy for heat requires either solar collectors – a method known as active solar – or the integrated design of energy efficient buildings that trap solar gains passively – a method known as passive solar heating design.

Passive solar design in the UK

The space heating requirements of individual houses in the UK can be reduced by around 1,000kWh/year through the

4.1 *The Oxford Solar House designed by Sue Roaf and David Woods. The passive solar designed house has flat plate active solar collectors and 4 kWp of photovoltaic MC-Si modules on the roof.*

adoption of simple passive solar design (PSD) measures. More complex PSD measures can increase this to about 2,000kWh/year. If this was scaled up across the national housing market, the total energy and carbon dioxide savings could become significant.[1] Passive solar heating depends on an integrated design approach that positions the majority of glazing and the most frequently used rooms on the southerly side of the house; specifies high performance windows and includes high thermal mass to store solar heat gains. PSD principles must also be applied to the design and layout of whole housing estates to allow for unshaded solar access and correct orientation for as many of the houses as possible.

ETSU has estimated that unplanned use of sunlight in buildings already represents a contribution to space heating and lighting in UK buildings in the order of 145TWh/year (or 145,000 million kWh/year). The number of houses *specifically* designed to make use of passive solar energy is around 1,400 and these have a combined passive solar credit estimated at over 9,000MWh/year.[2]

Active solar systems

Solar collectors for delivering hot water are usually on a south facing inclined roof and the heated water is circulated to a hot water storage tank. There are two basic types of solar collectors:

- The flat plate collector has a black coated absorber, a glazed front and insulated rear. Flat plate solar collectors can be integrated into roof construction.
- The evacuated tube collector has an absorber consisting of a pipe inside an evacuated glass tube which greatly improves efficiency. These are more efficient than the flat plate type of collector but are more expensive.

Solar water heating systems of a few square metres in area can provide two thirds of the hot water requirements of a household in the UK. However, because heating fuels have been relatively inexpensive, there has been no incentive to install solar water heating systems, though since the mid 1970s about 40,000 systems have been installed. The potential accessible resource for solar domestic hot water systems in the UK by the year 2025 is estimated to be 12TWh/year (or 12,000 million kWh/year) of which 9.6TWh/year is assumed to replace oil or gas and 2.4TWh/year electricity.

Another approach that has been shown to have some promise is solar aided district heating (SADH) systems. In summer, collectors heat a large quantity of water which is stored in a thermal store (usually an underground water tank) which is of a sufficient size to store the heat from summer to winter. Several such systems have been constructed in Scandinavia (which has shorter summers and longer winters than the UK), Denmark and Germany.

ETSU has estimated that with a construction rate of 150,000 new dwellings per year and SADH systems fitted to 50% of all new dwellings (from 1995 onwards), each with a heat load of 11,300kWh/year (and a 70% solar contribution), SADH systems would result in a potential accessible resource of some 18TWh/year by 2025.[3]

Photovoltaic solar electricity production

A different solar energy technology that has substantial potential for buildings in the UK is that of photovoltaic electricity generation using solar cells. Photovoltaic (PV) solar electricity generation using solid state solar cells has been around since the 1950s, but until recently it was so expensive that it could only be considered for use in remote locations or space craft. However, the cost has fallen by a factor of around 200 over two decades whilst at the same time module energy conversion efficiency has improved to 18%[4]. The manufacture of PV cells and modules is already a billion dollar industry worldwide. Even though PV-generated electricity is still much more expensive than conventional sources, it has become practical to consider integrating into buildings. The average house roof area in the UK is sufficient to generate electricity equivalent to the annual demand, particularly for a low energy house.

Types of PV cells and modules

Most PV cells are made from silicon in three basic forms: monocrystalline (MC-Si); polycrystalline (PC-Si); and amorphous (A-Si) thin film silicon. MC-Si modules are the most efficient (up to 18%) and the most expensive, PC-Si modules have efficiencies of 10% or more (but are less expensive than MC-Si), whilst A-Si modules have efficiencies of around 4–5% but are the least expensive type of solar cells. MC-Si modules were used on the University of Northumbria Solar Building, Oxford Solar House (Figure 4.1) and the Centre for Alternative Technology's PV building. PC-Si modules were installed at the Southwell Autonomous House and the Doxford Solar Office in Sunderland (Figure 4.2). A-Si modules were used on the BRE's Environmental Office of the Future (see Table 4.1). In addition to these established technologies, a number of new PV technologies are coming to market. Some of these offer significant reductions in cost and improvements in efficiency.

PV in buildings

PV can be integrated into buildings in the form of roof or

Table 4.1 Some examples of PV systems installed on UK buildings

Location/description

Commercial buildings	Position	Commissioned Year	Capacity kWp*
Newcastle – Northumbrian University Offices	facade	1994	40
Leicester – Beacon Energy Office	veranda canopy	1995	3
London – Thames Water Tower	feature	1995	0.3
London – Greenpeace offices	roof light	1996	0.7
Watford – BRE Environmental Office	facade	1996	2
Bridgend – Ford factory	roof lights	1998	105
Doxford – Solar Office	facade	1998	70
Domestic Buildings			
Southwell Autonomous House	pergola	1994	2.2
Oxford Solar House	integrated roof	1995	4
Brighton – 1 house	roof	1996	2.6
Milton Keynes – 9 houses	porch canopy	1996	18
Silvertown – 3 houses	roof	1997	3.3
Other			
Loughborough University – CREST Building	rack/roof	1995	2.2
Eversley – IT Power Test Centre	roof	1996	1.3
Homerton Adventure Playground Centre	roof tiles	1996	1.6
Southampton University	roof	1996	3.4
Leicester – Farm buildings	roof	1997	6
Machynlleth – Centre for Alternative Technology	roof	1997	13
Newport – West Wales Eco Centre	roof	1997	0.5

* kilowatts peak
Source: Taylor and Bruhns, 1999

wall cladding, roof tiles, glazing, roof lights and as solar shading devices. If costed on purely energy economic terms then PV is an expensive means of generating electricity, but when it comes to building costs clients often make choices not entirely based on economic criteria. Building integrated PV, unlike an expensive kitchen or car, can generate revenue or savings in the future.

For PV to be viable on housing it has to be straightforward to export and import electricity at no net difference in unit price as is the case in several European countries. This is not currently the case in the UK and is an additional barrier to PV installation. Current installed peak capacity from PV in the UK is over 500kW, but this is expected to exceed 1,000kW by the end of 1999.[5] PV is

4.2 *The Doxford Solar Office designed by Studio E Architects for Akeler Estates. It has 70kWp PV modules integrated into the sloping glazed facade which also provides passive solar gains.*

the principal renewable energy technology capable of generating electricity in the urban environment at the point of use and has great potential in the field of housing.

The European Parliament proposes a target of 3,000MW installed peak capacity in the 15 member states by 2010, largely provided by grid-connected building integrated systems. According to ETSU, building integrated PV technology is capable of meeting almost two thirds of the UK's annual electricity demand.

Wind energy

Wind energy is probably the most promising of all the renewable energy technologies suitable for use in the UK. Forty per cent of the European land based wind energy resource is located in the UK. The potential electricity production from wind power plant located at sites outside environmentally sensitive areas exceeds the current electricity production in the UK[6] (see Figure 4.3).

The wind energy available varies on a seasonal basis, peaking in the winter months which matches well the variations in energy demand for households. This is the reverse of solar energy which peaks in the summer months. Wind turbines are available in a range of sizes from very small devices capable of producing a few watts to large turbines with rated outputs of over 1.5MW. Most are installed in commercial wind power stations consisting of groups of turbines each rated at about 400kW or above.

Micro wind turbines (rated at a few watts) manufactured in the UK are relatively inexpensive and are used

4.3 *Accessible potential of electricity producing technologies in the UK (at bottom). Source: Adapted from REAG, 1992.[7]*

4.4 *A 225kW Vestas medium scale wind turbine at Wood Green Animal Shelter in Cambridgeshire.*

widely for charging batteries for boats and caravans. If the electricity requirement of a household is just a few low energy lights and very low power rated electronic equipment then it may be feasible to consider utilising one or more small micro wind turbines. Small scale wind turbines (larger than micro wind turbines and rated at a few kilowatts) are relatively expensive compared with medium scale wind turbines (on a per kilowatt basis), so it tends to be an expensive option to install a small wind turbine to supply an individual house.

More promising technically and economically is the use of a medium sized wind turbine (e.g. 200–600kW rating) as a community wind turbine. If the site is in a part of the country with sufficiently high wind speeds, it would in principle be possible to sell the excess electricity commercially to one of the regional electricity companies (RECs) or to one of the new green electricity schemes described later.

Most of the wind turbines operating in Denmark are owned and operated by locally owned co-operatives with Danish banks and building societies providing assistance for such projects. Two examples of an individual medium scale wind turbine are at the Wood Green Animal Shelter in Cambridgeshire and the Ashington Hospital in Northumberland. A medium scale turbine can produce enough electricity for many houses (the more energy effi-

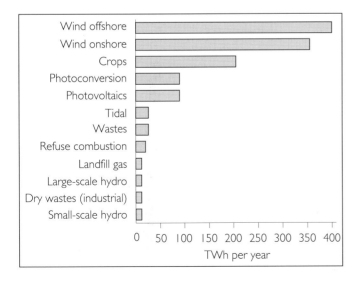

cient the houses, the more houses which can be served). An advantage of an estate turbine is that the costs can be shared between several householders.

Building integrated wind energy

In normal circumstances it is not advisable to install a conventional wind turbine on a building structure. However, the author and Altechnica are undertaking research into a new family of wind energy converters which use the building envelope as a means of enhancing and extracting energy from the winds blowing across their surfaces. These include the *Aeolian Roofs* and *Aeolian Towers*, *AeroSolar Power Towers* and also the *Aeolian Power Plane Turbines* (Figure 4.5).

4.5 *Aeolian Roof wind energy system.*

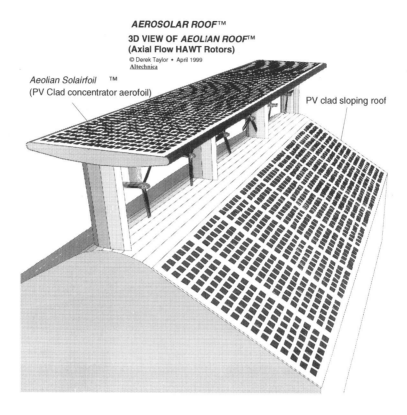

The Aeolian Roof utilises dual pitch or curved vaulted roofs in which the ridge is highly curved. A small distance above the ridge is located a wing like surface and devices for extracting energy from the wind are located in the opening between. The combination of roof shape and 'wing' induces an acceleration to the air flow enabling relatively small devices to extract more power. Initial calculations indicate that an Aeolian Roof is capable of generating a high proportion of the electricity requirements of a low energy house and if combined with PV roof cladding, a house could potentially achieve autonomy. The Aeolian Tower is similar to the Aeolian Roof except that it is vertically aligned and attached to the corner of a tall building. This potentially provides a means of generating hundreds of kilowatts of electricity in an urban environment.

Water power

Water power is much more site dependent than solar or wind energy and is not as widely distributed. Nonetheless if a fast moving stream or large river is situated in close proximity to a proposed housing project then there may be potential for water power exploitation. This will involve the installation of a water turbine coupled to a generator, but the type of turbine will depend on the 'head' (the height between the dam and the turbine) available, the volumetric flow rate, and whether there is to be a dam or whether a river current turbine is to be used.

Each water power installation usually requires a large amount of specially designed civil engineering works so there are no benefits from standardised mass production to keep the costs low. However, provided that there is sufficient water flowing through the system, it can be a very simple and straightforward means of generating electricity with no CO_2 emissions. Although the total potential is unlikely to be significant nationally (over 700MW capacity and over 3,000GWh/year electricity production potential)[8] most of the sizeable water power sites are already in use, but there is still potential for large numbers of small scale hydroelectric installations.

Geothermal energy

Geothermal aquifers

In the spa towns and certain other areas there is the potential to tap into geothermal aquifers which can provide heat for district heating systems. One such example is in Southampton. An 1800m deep bore hole at a city centre site provides hot water at 70°C and a district heat main delivers heat to the Civic Centre, Central Baths and several other buildings within a 2km radius of the bore hole.

Geothermal or ground source heat pumps

Even where there are not naturally occurring geothermal aquifers, heat can be usefully extracted from the ground over much of the UK. The temperature will not be as high as that in an aquifer, but by circulating water below ground level either via a horizontal coil or through a vertical bore hole (50 to 70m depth), low temperature heat can be extracted using heat pumps. Use of closed loop ground source heat pumps (GSHPs) is expanding rapidly in North America and in parts of Europe but they have not been widely used in the UK to date. It is estimated that there are between 250,000 and 350,000 units currently installed worldwide with an installation rate of approximately 45,000 per year.

Biofuels

Biofuels include fuels derived from organic municipal wastes, sewage, farm animal wastes, energy crops or crop and forestry residues. The potential accessible resource is estimated to be over 200TWh/year.[9] Unlike most other forms of renewable energy, biofuels can be stored for use when required, provided sufficient space is available.

To contribute to the energy requirements of a housing project, a local source of biofuels will need to be easily available. This may mean allocating part of a development area to growing energy crops (which could also be used as parkland) or contracting local producers to grow energy crops. It may also mean that the wastes from housing, such as sewage and organic matter, is converted into a usable fuel by biological treatment processing locally, although a large number of participating households would be required for

this to be feasible. On a large enough scale, domestic waste can be used for energy via digestion or combustion, or via processing into fuel pellets (refuse derived fuel).

For many reasons it often makes more sense to utilise biofuels in a neighbourhood or district scale combined heat and power (CHP) unit rather than in biofuel boilers or wood stoves for individual houses. The principal energy crops include coppiced willow (on a three to five year rotation) straw, rape seed oil and forestry wastes. All energy crops require large areas of land allocated to their production. Wood and straw based fuels can be used in special boilers for hot water or space heat provision. Alternatively these solid fuels can be 'cooked' in a gasifier (or pyrolysis unit) to yield a hydrogen rich gas that can be used to fuel a CHP unit to produce both electricity and heat. Vegetable oils can also be converted into a usable liquid fuel with minimal processing to produce a diesel fuel substitute known as biodiesel. This can be used to fuel diesel generator (or CHP) units.

The potential for biofuels in the UK is large but energy crops may come into land use conflict with land required for food crops unless an integrated approach is taken.

Green/renewable electricity schemes

The liberalisation of the electricity supply industry is creating opportunities for stimulating growth in electricity from 'green' or renewable energy sources. A number of schemes (over eight currently) have already been proposed and some are in pilot operation. They include the following types:

- contracting to supply electricity from guaranteed 'green' or renewable energy sources
- renewable energy surcharge for investing in renewable energy projects
- Green Pool electricity – which is currently fully subscribed
- Green electricity guarantee scheme and energy saving package

The *green electricity guarantee schemes* cannot guarantee that the electricity delivered to the consumer is

4.6 *Coppiced willow plantation.*

Other schemes

There are a number of opportunities for other schemes that can be established under the new liberalised regime, including *local renewable electricity schemes* – where the electricity is generated locally and used locally; and *community (or co-operative) renewable electricity schemes* where groups and organisations collaborate in producing the electricity.[10] It is also now possible for *local electricity (and heat) supply* companies to be established at a neighbourhood or district scale owned or partly owned by its customers. There could also be cross-sector partnerships established within a locality so that local businesses, farmers, educational establishments and local authority departments can be participants working in partnership with householders. It would also be potentially feasible for a local scheme (or inter-district partnership) to be established that installed renewable energy schemes elsewhere but utilised the grid as a conduit to 'transport' electricity to the housing site.

Conclusions

There are many opportunities to utilise renewable energy technologies in sustainable housing, but to achieve a significant contribution requires careful planning and commitment from the outset of a project's design phase. In many situations imaginative methods of financing may be needed until the approach becomes more commonplace.

If a new housing project is to be genuinely sustainable in energy terms and in avoiding CO_2 emissions it will have to utilise renewable energy, but it is also essential that the housing should be such that energy demand is considerably less than conventional housing built to current Building Regulations standards. If the energy demand of the households is not reduced, the size of the renewable energy equipment will be larger than it would otherwise need to be, making the project more expensive and less feasible.

However, when enough of a resource is available, there may be circumstances where it makes economic sense to install larger scale renewable energy equipment

coming from a renewable energy source but they do guarantee to generate an equivalent amount and feed it into the grid. Independent auditing agencies are being used to assure that the electricity generated is indeed from a renewable source.

The various *renewable surcharge schemes* are a kind of voluntary levy – around 10% – on subscribers' electricity bills. The funds raised in this way are guaranteed to be used to finance the development of new renewable energy projects selected by an independent advisory panel.

4.7 *A 25 kW gasifier for converting wood chips into a hydrogen rich gas.*

pays for electricity consumed. This approach avoids the capital equipment barrier that is often a stumbling block for investing in otherwise viable renewable energy technologies. A number of such schemes are being tried in The Netherlands, Germany and the USA.

There may often be circumstances that make it difficult to utilise renewable energy at or near a housing project site. Enabling housing in these circumstances to become more sustainable in energy and CO_2 terms may involve signing up with one of the new green electricity schemes. Alternatively, it may be possible to establish a local green/renewable electricity distribution scheme as part of the housing development (in which householders could be participants) and which could then contract other renewable energy producers to supply electricity to the scheme.

There are a number of investment funds available for developing renewable energy projects and if a scheme is viable it could stand a reasonable chance of obtaining investment. Also a number of banks are interested in supporting feasible projects and these could usefully be developed in the area of urban housing. Renewable energy is the key to long term sustainability.

References

1. ETSU, *The Potential Generating Capacity of PV Clad Buildings in the UK*, ETSU S 1365-P1, 1992.
2. ETSU, *An Assessment of Renewable Energy for the UK*, HMSO, 1994.
3. ETSU op. cit.
4. REAG, Renewable Energy Group Report to the Board of Trade, *Energy Paper 60*, DTI, HMSO, November 1992.
5. Taylor, D.A. & Bruhns, H. (1999) *Update of the Database of Photovoltaic Installations in the UK*, Altechnica for DTI, ETSU S/P2/00302/REP [In publication]
6. Taylor, D. (1996) 'Chapter 7: Wind Energy' in Boyle, G. (ed): *Renewable Energy: Power for a Sustainable Future*, Oxford University Press & Open University.
7. REAG op. cit.
8. Ibid.
9. Ibid.
10. Taylor, D.A. & Bruhns, H. (1997) *Maintenance of the UK Passive Solar Database*, Altechnica for DTI, ETSU S/P/00261.

to produce more electricity (or heat or fuels) than the housing needs. The excess energy could be exported and earn revenue which can then fund energy efficiency measures for the houses. This may be advantageous for existing housing that was not designed to particularly high energy performance standards.

It may also be possible to enter into partnership with utilities or energy companies to be the owners of renewable energy equipment (such as PV modules on householders' roofs, etc.) and in return the householder then

Chapter 5

Water conservation and housing

DAVID HOWARTH

The 27 water companies of England and Wales have recently submitted their latest demand forecasts to the Environment Agency. Whilst test projections indicate further and substantial reductions in leakage, these reductions are not sufficient to offset projected growth in household demand. The traditional response of the water industry to such a scenario has been to develop new water resources. In recent years, however, the political and regulatory climate has made this option less attractive, and ensured that the alternatives of water conservation and demand management have been placed firmly on the agendas of water companies.

Water use and demand forecasts

Currently in the UK for household use, average consumption of water is 150 litres per person per day. The rate of water use is rising whilst supplies, particularly in southern England, are falling. The Environment Agency has a duty to further 'sustainable development' which in the context of a renewable resource like water means keeping consumption within the limits of natural replenishment. As the House of Commons Environment Committee reminded us in 1996 'there is a responsibility upon those authorities, institutions and companies which are in a position to influence water usage ... to set an example'. This, of course, includes my own agency but also the construction professions who have such a big role to play in water conservation.

The abstraction of water goes mainly towards the public water supply (51%) but significantly to power generation (36%) and other industries including agriculture (13%). Although water used in power generation is

5.1 *The condition of water systems in towns is a good measure of environmental health. Falling water tables and pollution threaten the ecology of towns and countryside alike (top).*

5.2 *River Darent in Kent in stress from lack of rain (bottom).*

5.3 *Reservoir in drought. Half of all water is destined for use in buildings.*

returned close to the point of abstraction, about half of the power generated is used in buildings. Effectively, therefore, architects, engineers and developers influence directly and indirectly in excess of three quarters of all water consumption in the UK (more if leakage is included). Of the public water supply in 1997–98, 49.5% went to unmetered households and 4.4% to metered households. Although distribution leaks account for nearly 20% of the public water supply, water use still has to be a central theme of any national strategy towards sustainable housing.

Predictions suggest that with rising usage levels and with the present level of system leakage, new and potentially environmentally damaging water resources will be needed in the next century. It is not easy to be precise about the exact date because of the fluctuations in rainfall (due to climate change), the number, size and location of the 4.1 million new households needed by 2016, and the changing lifestyles of people within dwellings. But it is household demand that is driving the overall rise in water consumption, making water appliances and personal behaviour the critical factor in the water equation.

5.4 *Structure of water agencies in UK.*

Table 5.1 Public water supply 1997/98 (by volume)

Unmeasured household	49.5%
Measured non-household	24.4%
Distribution leakage	18.7%
Measured household	4.4%
Unmeasured non-household	1.6%
Other	1.4%

Source: OFWAT, 1998

The supply–demand balance

Three main strategies are available to balance supply and demand but each is constrained to some extent by cost, regulation and consumer resistance. The nation can either:

- develop new water resources (reservoirs, desalination plants, boreholes)
- increase demand management (water metering, low water using appliances, efficiency campaigns)
- adopt a combination of the above.

The approach should be one that considers the costs and benefits to society as a whole where such an analysis would include environmental and social aspects. At present, because of regulatory and political pressure, modest demand management coupled with the improvement of current infrastructure is the policy of most water supply companies. The development of new reservoirs or boreholes is expensive and difficult in planning terms and unlikely to gain support unless the demand management 'track' or the 'twin track' approach favoured by the government has been fully exploited.

Regulation

The water environment is one of the most regulated arenas in Europe with four major agencies responsible for different aspects of water supply or management in the UK.

Regulatory pressure has been responsible for ensuring that demand management and water conservation are firmly on the agendas of water companies. The Office of Water Services (OFWAT) is concerned with economic and pricing regulation, the Secretary of State DETR for setting the broad regulatory framework, the Environment Agency for environmental regulation, and the Drinking Water Inspectorate for regulating drinking water standards.

In the field of sustainable housing, there are two main aspects to consider at the outset:

- location – is there an adequate supply?
- design – what action can be taken to reduce demand?

Current planning guidance suggests that lack of water should not be a constraint on development. Water companies, with a duty to supply, are expected to transport it from elsewhere. Developers have been resistant to install water efficient appliances or to exploit water recycling.

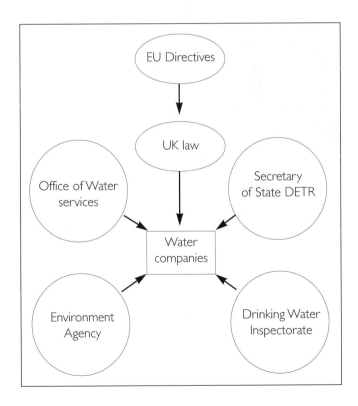

Table 5.2 Proposed changes to water use in Water Regulations in 1999

Appliance	1986 Water Byelaws	Proposed Regs
WC	7.5 litres/flush	6 litres/flush
Washing machine	150–180 litres/cycle	120 litres
Dishwashers	7 litres/place setting	4.5 litres/place setting
Showers	None	Meter if > 20 litres/min

Usually, architects and developers consider only demand reduction but they could exploit the supply side of the water equation by providing, for example, facilities for rainwater collection. However, it is in the field of water efficiency that cost effective benefits can be obtained. At present, water is relatively cheap but as scarcity bites in the future costs will rise. Even now in some parts of the country, water bills exceed energy bills for highly insulated houses. So it is prudent to design in water efficiency measures today in the expectation that over the life of the house, rising water costs will quickly pay for the initial increase in capital investment. Water conservation measures that can be taken in new homes include the following:

- low/dual flush toilets
- water efficient showers
- boilers that consider both water and energy usage
- collection at the building (rainwater)
- low water consuming washing machines and dishwashers
- avoidance of waste disposal units.

However, the choices affect lifestyles and whilst the Office of Water Services (OFWAT) and the Environment Agency believe that water conservation can be the least capital cost and best environmental option, many consumers and designers remain unconvinced of the wider benefits to water security.

The UK building and water regulations are relatively weak on water conservation. Compared with low energy design, water is rather taken for granted as a resource. The same was true until recently of the BREEAM assessment where again the emphasis was upon energy and other environmental factors but virtually excluding water. At the time of writing, changes to the UK Water Regulations are proposed and are expected to come into effect on 1 July 1999 (see Table 5.2).

Although water is now a key factor in the BREEAM assessment of housing at the design stage, the voluntary approach has not achieved significant change in practice in UK housing. The Environment Agency recognises four barriers to change:

- cost
- custom and practice
- customer desires (real or perceived)
- negative attitudes within the building industry.

Capital cost may be higher for a house designed to conserve water and the occupiers will also need to exercise restraint in certain areas (e.g. power showers, dishwashers). Also, the engineering of the house will be a little more complicated with more complex controls (e.g. water recycling) but there will be reduced water charges, the house will be more environmentally friendly, and the designer or developer can reflect upon the enhanced professionalism of the service. After all, ecology and ethics are at the root of the concept of sustainable development.

At present, it is possible at little or no additional capital cost to achieve a significant reduction in water consumption by the means outlined in Table 5.3. For the planned 4.1 million new homes required by 2016, they together add up to a saving of 1435.2Ml/day or 325 litres/house/day (based on an occupancy of 2.5). The water required for one house with no water saving measures could almost supply two houses with the water saving measures installed.

5.5 *Water use in buildings – shower.*

5.6 *Water use in buildings – bathroom.*

5.7 *Water use in buildings – washing machine.*

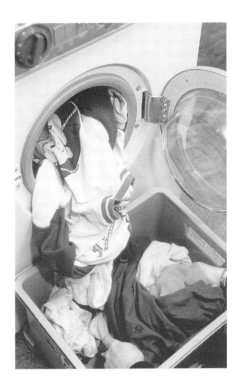

Table 5.3 Comparison of inefficient and efficient use for household appliances in 4.1 million new homes

Appliance	Comparison	Saving Ml/day
WCs	7.5 litres/flush vs 6 litres/flush	69.3
Showers	15 litres/min vs 3 litres/min	744.5
Washing machines	80 litres/cycle vs 50 litres/cycle	92.4
Dishwashers	27 litres/cycle vs 20 litres/cycle	20.0
Combi-boilers	"Instantaneous" hot water vs conventional	440.0
Waste disposal units	Unit vs no unit	69.0
Total saving		1435.2

Conclusions

Water conservation is a key factor in achieving sustainable development. Since housing uses over 50% of all abstracted public water supplies there are obvious benefits in exploiting design and management improvements in order to help conserve supplies. Water is an essential component of healthy living and a significant indicator of quality of life, but often water is wastefully used in the home and opportunities for recycling or rainwater collection are not taken. Even by specifying readily available low water consuming appliances as opposed to 'business as usual' appliances, a saving of 325 litres of water per household per day can be made. Water tomorrow, like oil today, will be a valuable resource under the pressures of an increasing number of households, growth in per capita use of water, and the uncertainties of climate change.

6

Sustainable housing: the Dutch experience

CHIEL BOONSTRA

The Dutch government was the first in Europe to adopt the principles of the Brundtland Report of 1987. It formed the basis for national energy and planning policy leading to the:

- National Environment Policy Plan, 1990
- Annex Plan on Sustainable Building, 1990
- Action Plan 1 on Sustainable Development, 1995
- Action Plan 2 on Sustainable Development, 1997.

The four plans established the local political agenda for sustainability in The Netherlands and came with a collection of grants, tax incentives and direct government support for demonstration projects.

The main agencies established since 1990 to implement the strategy for sustainable development are the:

- Environmental Council for the Building Industry
- NOVEM (government agency to promote energy research and implementation)
- SEU (to lead experiments in housing)
- SBR (to lead research into new building methods).

Collectively these four agencies, working with public and private interests, have the task of evolving, testing and implementing projects in support of more sustainable patterns of living in The Netherlands.

Sustainable development for the Dutch building industry has slightly different characteristics to that in the UK. There is greater emphasis given to three key areas:

- lifecycle impact of construction on energy, materials, water and land

6.1 *Masterplan of Ecolonia near Alphen aan den Rijn by Lucien Kroll. Notice the lake in the centre and the use of mainly terraced houses. The town tests various ecological approaches to design and construction.*

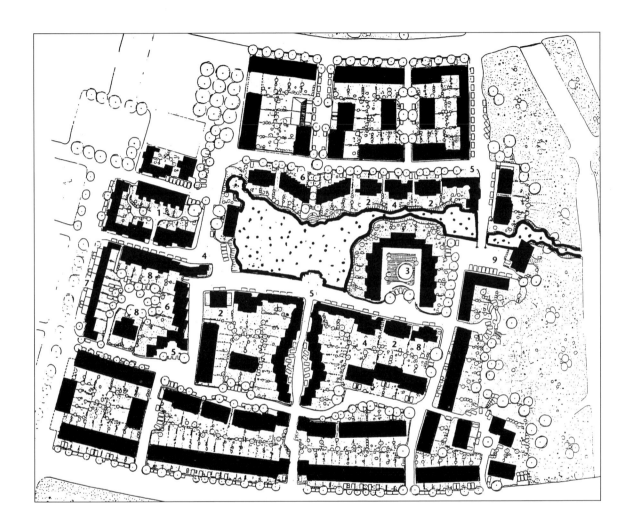

6.1 *Masterplan of Ecolonia near Alphen aan den Rijn by Lucien Kroll. Notice the lake in the centre and the use of mainly terraced houses. The town tests various ecological approaches to design and construction.*

- improvement to indoor air conditions, especially where health and comfort are concerned
- ecological infrastructure, especially the preservation and creation of habitats to sustain building.

In some ways the smaller population of The Netherlands, compared with Britain, France or Germany, and the greater development density has encouraged the focus upon questions of sustainability. With 15 million people and 6 million households on a land area only twice the size of East Anglia, the Dutch need to plan ahead. Moreover, an economy where only 6% are unemployed

and economic growth remains steady at about 2.5% per year results in the opportunity to think beyond political timescales. For example, in 1996 the government announced a programme of constructing 1 million houses over a 15-year period and declared that these had to be sustainable. That is why ambitious housing plans have been put in place and why also a great deal of testing is currently in progress. The government realises that to be sustainable there will need to be environmental innovation in the new housing. You cannot replicate mistakes a million times as the UK government did with its state sponsored housing in the 1960s.

6.3 *Houses in Ecolonia spread*
to the lakeshore which uses
reedbeds to purify the greywater
(opposite).

The Dutch government accepts its central role in achieving sustainable housing. It does not think that market forces will deliver in any area where the benefit is more global than personal. The mechanisms to drive change address a wide spectrum of the construction industry. Central government uses local authorities to create a 'demand' for green housing via the planning system and its ability to control development that is unsustainable. District plans have to include a percentage of sustainable housing and set targets for energy use which (unlike in the UK) is now seen as central to Dutch development planning. Areas of land in the district plans set aside for innovative approaches to sustainable housing are subject to developer and contractor competition. The competition system encourages interest in the topic and provides an opportunity to develop alternative ways of achieving sustainability. Also, since developers are perceived as being close to customers, it also ensures that new green ideas are feasible in terms of market expectations.

The system of setting targets for sustainability in national and local plans means that clients can reasonably demand higher environmental standards in the expectation that sustainable housing will be provided. The effect is to further push the Dutch building industry in the direction of sustainability with the result that architects, engineers and planners in The Netherlands are well versed in new green technologies. In fact, looking at Europe as a whole, it is fair to say that The Netherlands is at the forefront of sustainable housing construction and our examples, such as Ecolonia at Alphen, provide useful lessons for others.

By directing from the centre, the Dutch government has ensured that there are integrated design strategies in the field of sustainable housing. The testing of different types of solution, the dissemination of results, the development of

new ecological auditing systems, collectively help to promote the sharing of experience around holistic solutions. Conferences on sustainable construction are commonplace and many are organised by universities (such as that at Delft) which are at the forefront of research on sustainability. Unlike I suspect in the UK, the universities and private research consultancies such as my own, receive direct grants to test new approaches to sustainable development.

One of the key tools employed to monitor sustainable housing is the improved Energy Performance Standards contained in the Dutch Building Codes. The target is to achieve a 30% efficiency improvement in CO_2 emissions by building type over a 10-year period – new housing, offices, schools and shops. Lower standards apply to existing buildings where energy efficiency enhancement is harder to achieve, though arguably more important statistically. The targets add a welcome air of transparency to energy auditing, giving for instance house purchasers a chance to compare energy performance of different house types in advance.

Besides energy, the government sponsored *Handbook of Sustainable Building* lists other indicators of sustainable development, also setting targets for improvement. To understand the complex interactions in design choices a system of lifecycle assessment known as Eco-Quantum has been developed. It is an assessment tool that looks at functional units of construction (walls, windows, etc.) and measures likely impacts against ecological, environmental and energy indicators. What is important about the system is its comprehensive yet integrative nature; it is especially useful for building designers. The building lifecycle costs are quantified against key indicators such as emissions, recycling opportunities and waste. Under the system, sustainability issues such as health, pollution, toxic emissions and

The green context

6.4 *Solar thermal collectors used on the roof of an existing housing block in Zaandam as part of energy upgrading.*
Architect: Hans van Heeswijk

6.5 *Modest but acceptable social housing at Den Haag which integrates various strands of Dutch thinking on sustainability.*
Architct: Splinter Architecten Den Haag

global impacts are highlighted in a fashion that can influence material or design choice. Again, it was the government that helped develop the Eco-Quantum approach because it felt uneasy about auditing methods that relied solely upon energy as an indicator of sustainable development.

Enhanced environmental performance standards are crucial to the realisation of sustainable housing, but architects should not forget that sustainability creates better communities. There is an important social dimension to sustainable development which, with the emphasis upon energy, is easy to forget. But if you pursue the environmental priorities outlined earlier, there is no doubt that sustainable housing will be both distinctive in form and socially cherished. Only if it is robust and enduring (culturally, environmentally and socially) will housing be truly sustainable.

Mention was made earlier of fiscal policy in favour of sustainable housing. There are tax incentives through a Green Investment Bank, which also provides mortgages for sustainable projects. The bank, which is partly government owned, offers an advisory service to companies and individuals. It also assists developers in attracting grants from elsewhere (such as EU Thermie grants) and is the main agency underwriting the 100 or so energy projects currently on site in The Netherlands. It was the Green Investment Bank that carried the risks for the development of the Lucien Kroll master-planned village of Ecolonia aan den Rijn. Working with private house builders and the different architectural practices, Ecolonia successfully tested a variety of novel approaches to sustainable design within the field of lower to middle income housing.

The existing stock of housing is less easy to tackle from a sustainability point of view than new construction. We made many mistakes in the reconstruction of Dutch towns, creating poorly built, energy inefficient, socially divisive housing schemes. The challenge today is to modify the estates to make them more sustainable without actually pulling them down. Energy enhancement is the key to estate remodelling and in the process of improving efficiency we will raise comfort levels and make the housing blocks more visually attractive. Several projects are currently on site and others that have been completed are now being monitored. Three main initiatives are being

taken to cut CO_2 emissions per household: first, the use of roof mounted solar collectors; second, the glazing in of open, high level balconies; third, a trial scheme of photovoltaic over-cladding of poorly insulated blocks. Most existing social housing schemes have been double glazed, with the insulation levels raised in wall and roof, but more remains to be done to meet the national energy targets set in Action Plan 2 on Sustainable Development (1997).

Although it is expected that 80% of new houses will meet the new minimum standards of energy efficiency contained in the Building Codes by 2000, the existing housing stock remains a problem. The challenge is to evolve new ways of upgrading houses and estates, enhancing in the process the sense of social cohesion and improving the appearance of housing areas. What is good about sustainability is the opportunity it provides to create visual richness and to bring nature back into our cities. And as regulating standards rise under the influence of international obligations, such as the Climate Change Protocol signed in Kyoto, the potential to use our skills as architects and engineers is enhanced.

7

Transforming the existing housing stock: a strategy for achieving minimum standards of thermal comfort

PETER F. SMITH

In 1974, it was stated by the charity Shelter that in the mid-1970s Britain was almost the top of the league in terms of the proportion of GDP spent on housing. By 1994, investment had dropped to near the bottom of the league and things are not much better as the century closes. Over 7 million households are still, in 1999, below the official fuel poverty level. Bad housing has a profound impact on health. In the UK over £1 billion a year is spent by the health service on illnesses directly resulting from cold, damp and mould in housing. In 1980, the Labour government commissioned the eminent physician Sir Douglas Black to investigate if there was a link between poverty and ill health. His report published in 1980 established the link beyond doubt. It was binned by the incoming Tory government but has been resurrected by the Labour Secretary of State for Health. Recent research by London University into why the winters in Siberia did not increase mortality came up with two reasons: the inhabitants wore warm clothes and their living rooms were heated to around 20°C even when outside temperatures were as low as −48°C. In Britain, the fuel poor, many in private rented accommodation, endure much lower indoor temperatures.

The official government threshold for reasonable energy efficiency is SAP 60. The Standard Assessment Procedure (SAP) is made up of a calculation of the rate of heat loss resulting from the form of a building, the thermal properties of its fabric and the level of ventilation. This is

7.1 *Existing housing should be the focus of energy attention.*

equated with the cost of making good the heat loss via the heating system and the cost of the fuel used, taking into account any solar gains.

It has been criticised for including the fuel price because it is such a variable. Far better to have a system that focuses on the thermal efficiency of the fabric, plus space and domestic water heating systems. However, it is the official yardstick and will have to suffice.

Whilst the official base line for energy efficiency is SAP 60, the overall average for England is SAP 35. This is pushed up by post-1970s housing that has had to incorporate insulation. In the private rented sector, the SAP average is 21.7 with 26% below SAP 10. A significant num-

ber of the <10 group are as low as SAP –25. If Scotland and Wales were included the overall average would drop by a significant margin. All this adds up to a serious deficiency in terms of the quality of the UK housing stock and also explains why 27% of the CO_2 emissions in the UK are attributable to housing. If we build the 4.1 million new homes that are said to be needed by 2016, this will add a further 4 million tonnes of carbon to the UK total per year. Incidentally, as our nuclear power stations are decommissioned, if the shortfall is met by gas powered generation, this will add another 4 million tonnes to the atmosphere per year; the coal fired alternative would add about 8 million tonnes.

7.2 *Fuel poverty is worse in inner city areas such as here in the East End of Glasgow.*

Mention is made of these figures because the government has made a commitment to reduce CO_2 emissions by 20% by 2010 against 1990 levels. In my opinion, the only way there is any chance of meeting this target is by a radical thermal upgrading programme for the housing stock below SAP 65. Our initial estimate is that this would cut CO_2 emissions by 50%, which translates into a 15% reduction of the UK total. In the light of this claim, I and my colleagues have been given research funding by the government to work out how this target could be reached in what seems an impossibly short timescale. Here are some initial conclusions.

A thermal retrofit strategy

If this target is to be achieved there will have to be a systematic national programme underpinned by government regulation and funding. The present piecemeal approach to energy efficiency with its excessive deference to free market principles has no chance of reaching this 50% CO_2 reduction target. The barriers to a systematic programme of action at present are:

- a high percentage of owner occupiers, especially in England, plus private tenants requiring voluntary participation
- under the Home Energy Conservation Act, local authorities are obliged to state how they will raise the energy efficiency of housing within their boundaries by 30%. There are wide variations in methodology and quality of outcome under the Act
- the method of accounting employed by the UK Treasury focuses on capital spending and excludes revenue benefits. It is currently not able to offset capital costs with revenue gains and this distorts the cost effectiveness of capital intensive programmes
- there are serious discrepancies between official design parameters (i.e. Building Research Establishment Domestic Energy Model: BREDEM based) for household energy consumption and the actual energy consumption within lower efficiency housing
- the widening income gap and the rising proportion of the elderly is increasing the rate of fuel poverty. This will get worse as state pensions decline in real terms
- there are serious doubts about the capacity of the construction industry to deliver a rapid retrofit programme
- where local authorities have undertaken their own retrofit programmes, they have encountered serious problems of quality control
- the energy regulators' powers are currently confined to keeping down fuel prices and maximising market freedom.

If a national programme is to be successful within a market economy with a high proportion of home owners, then it has to offer both short term and long term benefits. The long term benefits are no problem, especially for low income, low SAP households where space heating costs might be reduced by 75–80%. The short term benefit would be achieved where the cost of energy plus repayments for the fabric upgrading would add up to less than the previous annual costs of energy alone. The problem here is establishing a benchmark for the

7.3 *Average difference between actual and expected energy consumption within SAP categories. Source: Unpublished PhD thesis by Chris Goodacre, University of Lancaster, 1997*

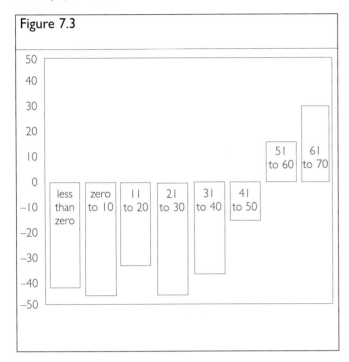

Figure 7.3

7.3 *Average difference between actual and expected energy consumption within SAP categories. Source: Unpublished PhD thesis by Chris Goodacre, University of Lancaster, 1997*

real annual energy costs. The standard computer model for the heat regime assumes a living room temperature of 21°C and 18°C for the rest of the house. The England House Condition Survey 1991 shows no average temperatures for living rooms reaching this average. An intensive localised survey in Lancaster by our research associate Chris Goodacre reveals a similar pattern when focusing on energy consumption and SAP rating 1. Only when SAP 51 is reached does energy consumption reach the level assumed by the standard heat regime model (see Figure 7.3).

The rationale for a large scale retrofit programme is that it should represent *realistically calculated* energy savings which will form the base line of a cost benefit equation. Therefore, it is essential that retrofit programmes be based as near as possible on actual energy costs rather than theoretical models. This means assessing costs on an area sensitive basis and fine tuning them to establish specific yardsticks at neighbourhood level.

Opinion is converging on the belief that the Energy

Service Company (ESCO) approach is the most likely mechanism able to realise the goal of radically improving the national housing stock. The principle behind an ESCO is that it supplies both energy and energy conservation services, such as improving the thermal efficiency of the building fabric and providing advice regarding fittings and appliances. The householder would receive a single bill for fuel and repayments for the upgrading costs. A KPMG report of February 1998 offers a commercially viable framework for ESCOs.[2] Estate models have shown that the housing stock requires an average investment of £5,000 per dwelling to achieve significant thermal improvements by means of measures such as over-cladding and double glazing. The market rate of return for the ESCO against this cost would be in the region of £800 per year for 14 years. For the householder, this cost would be offset by the cost of saved energy.

In order to provide an incentive to participate in the programme, householders should be assured of about a 10% saving in real annual costs embracing energy and energy services. The difference of about £500 per year should be met in the early years by government subsidy. If retrofit repayments were reduced at the outset but designed to track inflation, then government subsidy would taper and eventually disappear. In times of severe economic constraint, there would have to be a rigorous appraisal of the balance between costs and revenue. At a recent debate (May 1998) Lord Ezra, past Chairman of the

Table 7.1 Cost saving per year by type of house assuming 50% improvement in energy efficiency

Owner occupier	£375
Private rented	£309
Council tenants	£260
Housing association tenants	£230
Average for all households	£330
	prices £s sterling

Derived from the English House Condition Survey, 1991, DOE

7.4 *Improved and unimproved council flats side by side. The energy benefits of retrofit programmes include job creation and re-skilling of the workforce as well as CO_2 reduction. Architect: Assist (Glasgow)*

Coal Board, argued strongly in favour of retaining the levy on electricity, known as the Non-Fossil Fuel Obligation (NFFO). In effect this was a carbon tax that has largely been channelled into nuclear energy. The 10% levy should continue to operate since it is a tax to which consumers are accustomed but in future would embrace all fossil fuels. It should be ring-fenced to contribute to the year-on-year subsidy for the home upgrading programme. The government has shied away from overt carbon taxes for fear of electoral penalties. In a MORI poll conducted in October 1996, 66% of the British public supported the continuance of the NFFO with most believing it should be exclusively devoted to environmental causes. Such a programme will produce a steady increase in revenue benefits which will include:

- a boost to the construction industry. One new skilled job is created for every £30–35,000 spent on retrofitting buildings. Added to this will be up to one job for every £60,000 due to the re-spend factor. The support industries will also experience a significant increase in turnover. Within an industry with a high unemployment rate, this will have the added benefit of replacing unemployment benefit with tax and social security revenue

- the £1 billion annual health costs attributed to poor housing should taper off and there should be a marked reduction in deaths caused by hypothermia

- as less personal income is consumed by energy, this may well have an impact on the social benefits burden

- there will be extra disposable income through the cost of saved energy providing a further boost to the economy
- the capital value of the stock is significantly increased, with benefits both to the individual owner and the national stock value
- improved housing will mean a longer life expectancy with the effect of reducing the environmental costs associated with demolition and replacement
- according to the Oxford University Environmental Change Unit the final outcome of the balance between costs and revenue gains will be a net profit to the Exchequer. One of the facets of our research is to test this hypothesis.

Operation and management

For a scheme on a national scale, the operational structure will need to be centrally imposed. An existing quasi-government agency exists in the form of the Energy Saving Trust (EST). It would make sense for the Trust to be enhanced to provide oversight of the system and be accountable directly to government for the efficient operation of the scheme. The obvious next tier is the local authority. LAs would be responsible for delivering the target SAP for their area within the defined timescale and for achieving a minimum of, say, 75% uptake across all households. A member of the EST might be positioned within each LA for the duration of the operation. The government agency to which that EST person would report would be the regional office of the Department of the Environment, Transport and the Regions (DETR). The regional structure of the DETR suits well the geographical obligations under the proposal.

The operational responsibility should be vested with specialised project management companies that have demonstrated their capability in this sphere. They would be responsible to the LA for completing the work to specification and on time.

The LAs would typically be required:

- to assess the real costs of energy to households as the median between highest and lowest within a given neighbourhood

- building on data gathered under the terms of the Home Energy Conservation Act (HECA) to assess the work needed within contract boundaries to raise the minimum SAP to 65. The work would be based on nationally agreed specification standards
- to identify ESCOs that would be willing to tender within the LA area. These would be checked for in-house expertise, etc
- to select a short list of project management companies
- to publicise the programme within their area and obtain a sample of likely uptake rate from owner occupiers, private tenants and housing association tenants. LA tenants would be included automatically
- provide temporary accommodation for temporarily displaced vulnerable residents (elderly, sick, etc.).

The LAs would then seek tenders from approved ESCOs which would include:

- the cost of electricity and gas fixed for the duration of the contract unless the market dropped by over, say, 5% in which case the ESCO price would track the rate of reduction; increases in price would not be passed on to consumers
- the cost of upgrading individual properties according to the specification provided by the LA and to a standard of at least SAP 65
- the duration of the contract, including penalties for delays
- guarantees of security of supply of energy.

Once the contract terms had been agreed, the LA would appoint the accepted project management company tenderer.

The way forward

For this strategy to be possible, a number of things will need to happen. First there will have to be changes in the regulations governing the primary responsibilities of the fuel regulators if ESCOs are to function effectively. At present, consumers have a statutory right to change energy suppliers at 28 days' notice. Since the supply of energy and energy efficiency services would be offered as a single package, it will be necessary for consumers to agree to be locked-in to the ESCO for the duration of the contract. This degree of market stability together with economies through long term financing packages will enable ESCO to offer a highly competitive energy price at the outset.

The government seems to be creating a political climate in which it would be acceptable to override the duties of the regulators to maximise market freedom where ESCOs are involved in large scale retrofit programmes. At the same time, the regulators would have powers to ensure that ESCOs did not take advantage of customers. A recent government Green Paper appears to be creating the regulatory climate to allow ESCOs to operate:

'Where Ministers wish to implement social or environmental measures, including energy efficiency measures, which have significant financial implications for consumers ... these should be decided by Government and implemented through new, specific legal provision rather than through guidance to the regulators.'[3]

Where necessary an LA should provide temporary accommodation for households for whom the disruption would impose an unacceptable burden on an inhabitant, such as the elderly and chronically sick.

Reference was made earlier to the skills shortage within the construction industry. This is especially acute in the sphere of retrofit energy efficiency technologies. It will be necessary to embark on a national crash programme of education and training to ensure there is a qualified workforce that increases in parallel with the demands of the industry. We could learn from the Swedish government's two year intensive training programme in advance of the introduction of stricter energy regulations under SBN 80, which ensured there were sufficient expert operatives to cope with the rigours of the greatly enhanced thermal standards.

Conclusion

Upgrading the housing stock is the most effective way of achieving significant CO_2 reductions by 2010 whilst also realising social and economic benefits. There must also be radical changes in the supply side of energy provision with much more resources targeted at renewable energy and CHP. However, the central message of this chapter is that if we are to stem the onward march of global warming and climate change then we must be prepared to carry the costs and to accept limits to our individual freedom. The strategy described will only work if domestic customers accept that their freedom to play the energy market at short notice would be suspended during the period of an ESCO retrofit programme. Surely this is not too much to ask, especially as householders will experience immediate benefits. Yet this small problem symbolises the global dilemma. All the economic trends are in the direction of the free market and deregulation, whilst the environmental thrust is towards regulating the market so that it contributes to the security of the planet. This security is especially threatened by the failure so far to halt the rise in CO_2 emissions. The simple truth is that saving the planet in the long term is not compatible with free market economics. From the market perspective, saving the planet is simply not cost effective.

Perhaps salvation lies in 'the third way' or *via media* between command economics and the unfettered market. One thing is certain, the problems stemming from poor housing will not be solved without vigorous government intervention.

References

1. Chris Goodacre, unpublished PhD thesis, University of Lancaster, 1997.
2. The KPMG report is summarised in *What Price Energy Efficiency*, Energy Saving Trust, February 1998.
3. *A Fair Deal for Consumers* Department of Trade and Industry, 1998, paragraph 2.3.

Case studies

8

A design methodology for urban sustainability: three case studies

ANDREW WRIGHT

A properly integrated design approach can maximise social opportunity and enhance the quality of urban areas. Integration of professional input, if followed from the outset, gives clarity and structure to new urban solutions around the emerging priorities of sustainable development. Housing form and layout should be generated by the need to achieve simple social pleasures: such as having access and views to attractive gardens; each home should have good orientation for solar gain so that living spaces have a pleasant and warm ambience for the family to enjoy; in urban areas each home should be connected to a good transportation system that is prioritised to people; and above all, there should be linkage to a clear framework of supporting community facilities.

Provision of such social and environmental commodities is essential in all new design proposals. Omission should be seen as a failure, rather than their inclusion being regarded as a commendable luxury as often happens today. Architects, planners, developers and housing authorities should be accountable for their inclusion rather than their exclusion.

An integrated approach to design gives definition and character to form, whether in rural or urban settings. However, independent consideration of issues such as solar gain or transportation can induce a repetitive, unimaginative environment.

Juxtaposition, association and weighting of all the sustainability issues is essential. The resulting design within each specific contextual framework should be rich and delightful, embodying a natural order that links into other priorities in the project. These orders then coalesce into a whole with synthesis of form based upon the sustainability agenda.

8.1 *View of typical room at the Holy Island Monastic Retreat. Architect: Andrew Wright Associates*

Three projects

This chapter focuses on three specific projects: a Buddhist community on Holy Island in Scotland; a design proposal for a sustainable community on the Greenwich Millennium Village site; and the masterplan of an urban village in Wolverhampton. The projects have been designed by Andrew Wright Associates (AWA) in close collaboration with engineers and consultants such as Ove Arup and Partners, BDSP, Battle McCarthy and Grant Associates.

Holy Island

The Holy Island project originated in an open international design competition. The AWA design was shown at the Royal Academy and received an award in the Summer Exhibition. AWA were then asked by the client to develop the idea further, testing the feasibility of the approach. The project has now received planning permission. The site, near to the Isle of Arran off the west coast of Scotland, has a long history as a sacred place and was purchased by the

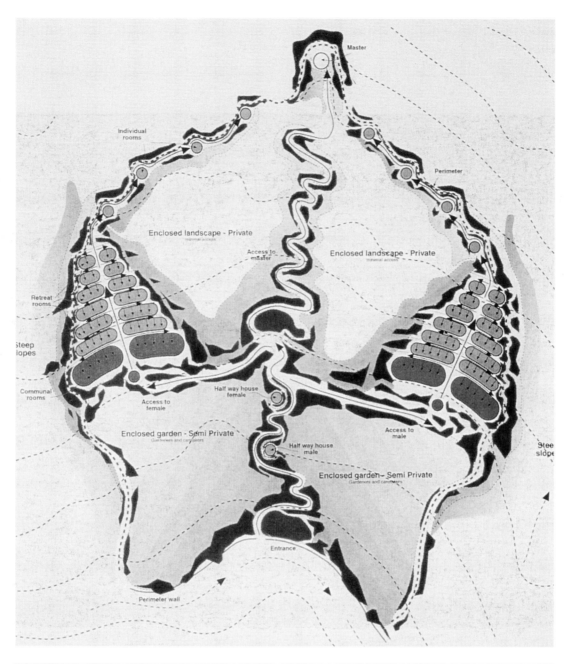

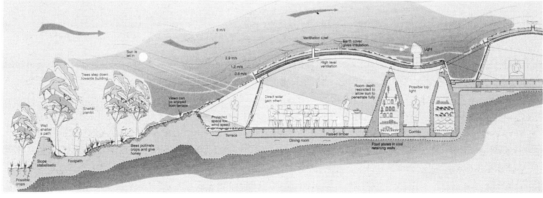

8.2 *Site plan (top) and section
(bottom) of the Holy Island Retreat
in Scotland.
Architect: Andrew Wright Associates*

8.3 *Conceptual basis for road layout
at Greenwich Millennium Village.
Architect: Andrew Wright Associates*

Rokpa Trust in 1992. Their aim was to build a Buddhist retreat centre, to create a focus of peace, environmental sustainability and inner faith activity on this beautiful remote Scottish island.

The centre consists of 110 individual retreat rooms organised in two separate wings which sit either side of a small valley. Communal facilities are located at the entrance to the complex with the more private retreat rooms blending into the hillside in a reductive manner, so that privacy and a sense of silence is heightened. The whole complex nestles into the hillside with individual buildings partially sunk into the south facing slope to take maximum advantage of passive solar gain. The gently undulating roofs are planted and designed to deflect or reduce wind speed. The more exposed units at the bottom of the hill have the additional protection of an earth berm and shelter planting. The profile of the development is rounded in response to wind and in order to temper the visual and ecological impact.

The buildings are highly insulated and covered in earth to reduce heat loss and maintain relatively stable internal temperatures. Insulating shutters are used at night to further reduce heat losses. It is estimated that energy consumption will be reduced by two thirds compared with current norms for houses in similar locations.

A fundamental element in the design of the dwellings is the need to collect and conserve water. Rainwater for washing and cleaning is collected along a gully at the upper roof perimeter, and stored at the highest point of each retreat. Fresh water for drinking or food preparation is taken from natural springs. Rain falling on to buildings and the higher garden flows naturally into a central upper pond. Most waste water is naturally filtered through reed beds, and fed into a lower pond which forms a central focus at the entrance to the complex, and is used for irrigation of crops and would also serve as a hydrant in case of fire.

The reduction in energy of 70% is achieved by good orientation and energy efficient design. Remaining energy needs are generated by modestly scaled wind generators. We have positioned the turbines in an exposed position where they are more efficient, allowing their number to be reduced. This has helped in reducing overall visual impact and securing planning consent.

Greenwich

Our scheme for the Greenwich Millennium Village site was developed in an integrated professional fashion as an independent project outside the official competition. As masterplanners we were supported by sympathetic consultants such as Binnie Black and Veatch (engineering), Grant Associates on landscape and ESD on energy. The key was to exploit the competition brief which focused on a central landscaped park and to extend this via a series of green corridors which spiralled out to form a hub of new social neighbourhoods. These planted, in this demonstration design, effectively act as urban village greens to form the focus of community activity. We firmly believe that by integrating spatial, land use and landscape design with transport planning, a clearly defined sustainable urban structure emerges.

The denser node to the north west enjoys spectacular views of the River Thames and will form a hub for leisure activities such as restaurants, a yacht club, sports clubs and fashion shops. The area by the river to the east of the site provides buildings for businesses, and will also include shops, cafes and a town hall. Smaller nodes set further back in the site are quieter, and have a more residential character.

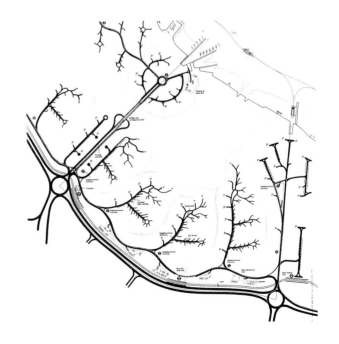

Case studies

8.4 *Amenity and ecological strategy at Greenwich Millennium Village. Demonstration design by Andrew Wright Associates*

8.5 *Model of Greenwich Millennium Village. Proposal by Andrew Wright Associates*

The ecology park to the south is intended to provide a diverse complex of wetland habitats of real value to wildlife, both resident and migratory. The park is designed to attract many species to the area that would not usually be seen in cities. We see the ecology park as an educational attraction for use by local schools, but also importantly, an accessible amenity for each new home on the site. The scheme structures the urban framework so that each home has direct access to parks and wildlife areas as well as views over them. Effectively the ecological network merges with the social structure to create an integrated whole.

A fundamental part of the competition brief for the Millennium Village was to strike a balance between residential, working and community facilities. Our proposed mix is 50% residential, 36% commercial and 14% public and community facilities, with a minimum of 1,000 homes being required to make the combination viable. Each neighbourhood includes commercial floor space, live/work units and some community facilities, in addition to housing. Family homes are located at the heart of each neighbourhood, protected by taller denser blocks around the perimeter.

Water conservation is a feature of our design at Greenwich. Recycling grey water results in the site being 30–35% more efficient in water use compared with current standards. The ponds and wetlands within the ecology park are also maintained by cleaned grey water from adjacent apartment blocks. The park depends upon recycled water for the maintenance of the water table which needs to remain high for reed growth.

The scheme relies on a centrally located public transport system. Trams are reached within five minutes' walk, and the local shuttle bus is no more than three minutes' walk from any point in the development. Vehicular circulation is restricted to the perimeter, feeding in to the neighbourhoods, and carefully laid out to reduce to a minimum traffic noise in residential areas. Individual houses have their own parking space. Communal parking areas, located at the entrance to each neighbourhood, provide peak capacity and shared parking for offices. Within each local area, priority is given to pedestrians and cyclists, and there is an integrated network of pedestrian and cycle routes with good links to the surrounding areas.

In terms of energy, the main strategy is to reduce

8.6 *Section through typical block.*
Architect: Andrew Wright Associates

8.7 *Bird's-eye perspective of*
typical housing area.
Architect: Andrew Wright Associates

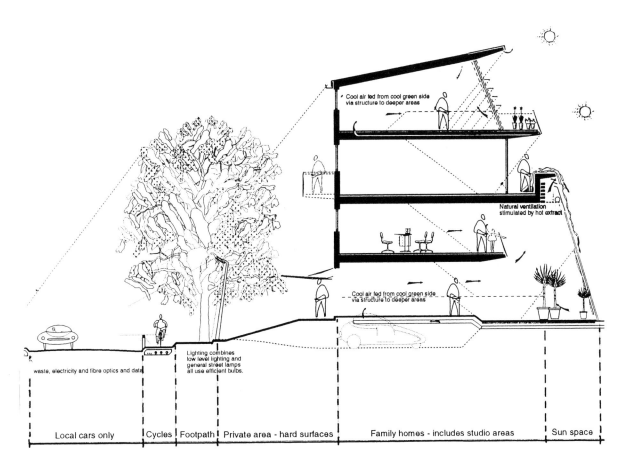

Cool air fed from cool green side
via structure to deeper areas

Natural ventilation
stimulated by hot extract

Cool air fed from cool green side
via structure to deeper areas

Lighting combines
low level lighting and
general street lamps
all use efficient bulbs.

waste, electricity and fibre optics and data

| Local cars only | Cycles | Footpath | Private area - hard surfaces | Family homes - includes studio areas | Sun space |

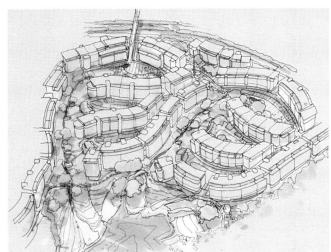

8.8 *Perspective sketch of Greenwich proposals.*
Architect: Andrew Wright Associates

8.8 *Perspective sketch of Greenwich proposals.*
Architect: Andrew Wright Associates

demand by using low energy design, then supply space and water heating by an efficient combined heat and power (CHP) plant. This would be fired initially by mains gas, but could eventually use biomass or wood chips transported by river, or household waste. Energy consumption and CO_2 emissions are calculated to be less than 30% of a conventional power station system, with the potential for zero CO_2 emissions using coppiced wood to supply the CHP plant (based upon CO_2/oxygen exchange during the growing stage).

Bilston Urban Village

Another project that tests sustainable design approaches is the Bilston Urban Village in the West Midlands, for Wolverhampton Metropolitan Borough Council acting jointly with English Partnerships. The project was awarded by open competition to AWA, leading a team that includes Ove Arup and Partners, Bucknall Austin, DTZ Pieda and Grant Associates. The site covers an area of approximately 70ha and has remained derelict because of the presence of over 180 mine shafts and extensive landfill. This gap in the urban fabric has resulted in disconnected local communities.

The design targets incorporated in the brief and resolved in the masterplan are to:

- remodel the central valley landscape
- restore Bilston Brook, and clean the nearby canal
- create a distinct central wetland landscape for amenity
- form a new social heart for the district
- include a mix of land uses to create 1,350 new homes and 3,000 new jobs
- provide good public transport systems
- use roads scaled to human needs
- conserve water supplies by 30%
- provide good solar access to every home
- achieve a planned energy saving of 70%.

Bilston is an exciting project. It creatively uses the large amount of earthworks and extensive remediation necessary on this site to remodel a central valley landscape in order to create a distinct high quality heart to the development.

Central to the positive response in the project from councillors, planners and local communities has been an extensive and full consultation process. Careful explanation of how a well integrated urban plan can promote social cohesion and create an exemplary environment for people has done much to achieve broad and enthusiastic endorsement.

8.9 *Model of Bilston Urban Village.*
Architect: Andrew Wright Associates

8.10 *Sketch of integrated*
transport at Bilston Urban Village.
Architect: Andrew Wright Associates

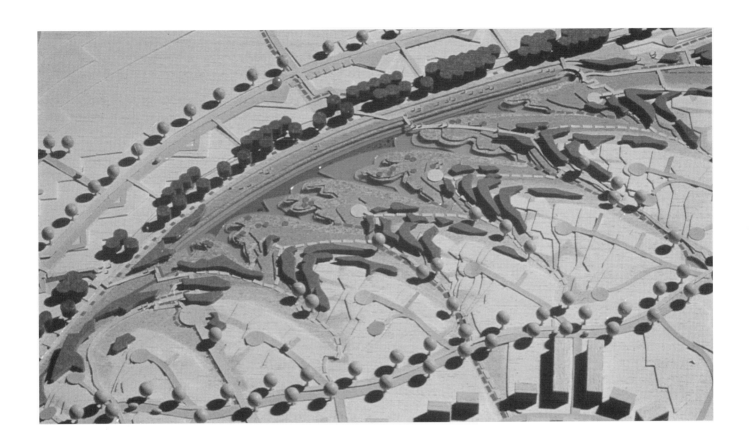

Whilst there is much more work to be done to develop and articulate the urban form itself, we are pleased we are managing to knit in a wide range of 'sustainable issues' into the general planning and layout of the village.

Lessons from the three projects

We advocate an 'integrated design process' that considers the 'full palette' of design and urban issues. Rather than constraining the design process, by a retrospective, additive process, intergration, if creatively fused from the onset, gives clarity, structure and delight to building and urban design.

Such a process is essential to sustainable development.

Greenwich Millennium Village: a case study of sustainable housing

BEN DERBYSHIRE

As a practice, HTA (formerly Hunt Thompson Associates) generally avoid design competitions, but were attracted to the Greenwich Millennium Village competition because of its aims: to demonstrate the full range of technical, social and economic options for sustainability on a high profile urban site alongside the Millennium Dome. In particular we were keen to work with mainstream developers in order to show that innovative techniques could be achieved within usual economic constraints. In this way the project would be a genuine demonstration of economic sustainability and technological innovation.

Our clients were Countryside Properties plc, Taywood Homes, Moat Housing Group and Ujima. We approached Ralph Erskine, the celebrated Scandinavian architect who had been an inspiration to our practice since the 1970s when he pioneered community architecture in this country at Byker in Newcastle. When we were thinking about who to collaborate with on the Greenwich project, his description of his own architecture as 'finding poetry in the economic use of resources' seemed to us to strike at the heart of our aspirations for the Millennium Village.

In our entry for the competition we wanted to show that it was possible in housing to emulate the degree of choice available in other markets. By providing housing of all tenures one can remove the stigma that is attached to 'social' housing, at the same time as offering something much more than the superficial 'kerb appeal' of the private sector. We see flexibility as the key to achieving this, by providing a wide range of choice for customers initially and then ensuring the potential for adaptability in the long term. Our proposal sought to demonstrate ways of creating an organic incremental approach to the provision of

9.1 *Aerial perspective of Greenwich Millennium Village designed by HTA and Ralph Erskine.*

9.2 *HTA/Ralph Erskine's masterplan for the Greenwich Millennium Village.*

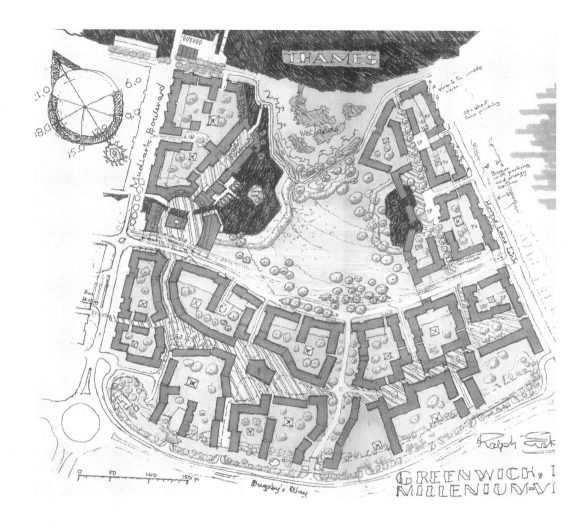

homes and communities that replicates the gradual processes of the past in a contemporary fashion.

Our entry for the Greenwich Millennium Village competition aimed to prove that by employing efficient construction techniques it was possible to make substantial cost savings. Apart from offering better value, factory based construction would provide the degree of flexibility in dwelling form and layout that in turn delivers choice. If residents can go on exercising choice within their environment, adapting it to their changing needs, designers can begin to make places where people want to be, and want to stay. Only then will real meaning attach to the term 'environmental sustainability'.

In our winning competition entry, we aimed to show how a first time buyer can purchase a small first floor flat over a workshop then extend it by adding a conservatory which could be purchased via a Management Trust (of which more later) using the economic benefits of bulk purchase. The Trust would also ensure a degree of aesthetic control over the process of growth and change. Eventually the flat could be extended downstairs to accommodate the needs of a growing family. In this way the initial residents, who are likely to be young people, will be encouraged to stay and adapt their homes rather than move away.

Our strategy was to adopt ambitious construction targets for the project: 25% reduction in construction time; 30% reduction in building cost; zero defects; high safety

9.3 *Green spine and light transit route looking towards village park. Architects: HTA and Ralph Erskine*

Table 9.1 Main design objectives and attractions at the Greenwich Millennium Village

- masterplan that works for people not cars
- virtual village and exhibition on aspects of sustainable urban communities using the Internet
- reinvention of village for urban living in 21st century
- revolution in the design of homes exploiting intelligent systems
- model of environmentally sustainable development
- new era in UK housebuilding based upon off-site prefabrication
- package of innovations that can be delivered

Table 9.2 Environmental targets at Greenwich Millennium Village

- 80% reduction in primary energy consumption
- 10% energy from wind and solar sources
- 50% reduction in embodied energy
- 30% reduction in water demand
- 50% reduction in on-site waste
- 80% recyclable building
- zero CO_2 emission

Table 9.3 Buildability targets at Greenwich Millennium Village

- 30% reduction in construction cost
- 25% reduction in construction time
- zero defects at handover

standards; and maximum waste reduction. Lessons learned from the commercial sector in terms of fast track construction would be adopted, particularly steel frame structures and prefabricated cladding systems. These innovation targets were to be achieved gradually over the course of the development in a planned process where feedback from each successive phase would be used to improve performance. The approach mirrors the recommendations of the Latham Committee but targeted here to the rigours of speculative housing.

Ralph Erskine's response to the masterplan for the whole Greenwich Peninsular by the Richard Rogers Partnership (incorporated into the competition brief) was to introduce the concept of 'external rooms'. This charac-

teristic response to microclimate issues adds amenity and (critically from the point of view of our developer clients) value to the development. Wind is a major constraint on the site and Battle McCarthy, our consulting engineers, have carried out an analysis to minimise its impact at ground level. This has generated a built form that rises from two to 12 storeys from south to north across the site to protect the residential areas from the cold north easterly winds that blow across the Thames. Buildings are designed to create a ramped effect making use of laminar flow to deflect south westerly winds and create a calm microclimate at ground level.

The energy strategy is based on a holistic approach, reducing demand by incorporating high levels of insulation and utilising the south facing slope of the site to take advantage of passive solar gain. The stepped built form allows the sun to penetrate sheltered courtyards and into the majority of dwellings. Supplementary energy supply is provided by a combined heat and power plant which was to have used bio-mass fuel.

9.4 *Typical apartment block,
north facade. Notice the mix of
types of accommodation at the
Greenwich Millennium Village.
Architects: HTA and Ralph Erskine*

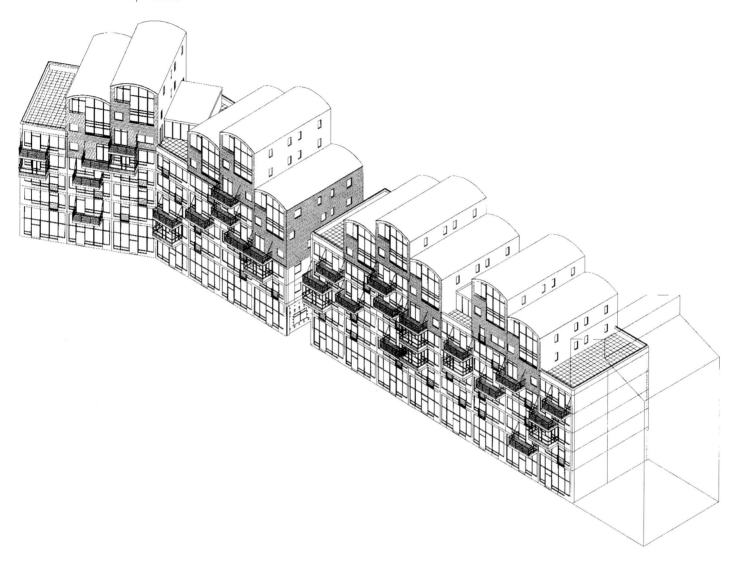

One of the most important issues incorporated into the masterplan is that of visual and social connectivity. As the site is bounded by two major roads and the river, we have worked hard to integrate the development into its surroundings with a network of sustainable means of transport: cycle and pedestrian routes; a light transit system running through the village; and the new Jubilee Line extension. These physical means of movement are linked to corridors of parkland which will ensure physical and perceptual integration.

The masterplan illustrates our approach to the segregation of vehicles and pedestrians and aims to reduce the visual impact of parked cars by locating them wherever possible in secure podium spaces under the landscaped courtyards. It was important to us that a development designed to express our aspirations for the next millennium should have an external environment that is virtually car free. A further aim of the masterplan is to create a variety of spaces that are sheltered and defined by buildings and which express a strong vernacular language. There are four distinct housing areas linked by a necklace of open spaces, offering variety and shelter. A more formal oval space lies at a critical point dividing the Southern Park from a linear park which leads towards the Dome. The

9.5 *Facade study - south elevation. Transparency has been moderated by extensive use of grilles at the Greenwich Millennium Village. Architects: HTA and Ralph Erskine*

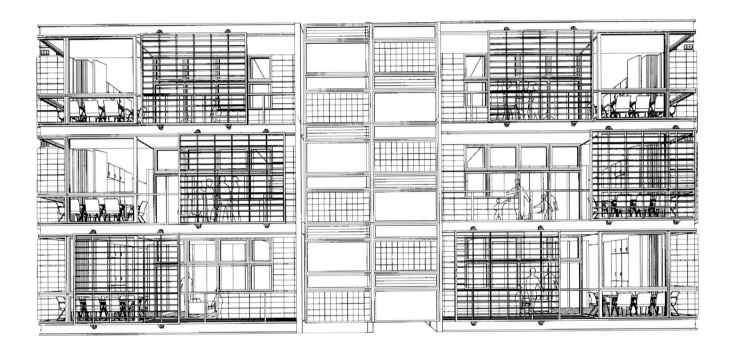

Southern Park, which includes an ecology area offering a wetland environment for migrating birds as well as a lake for human recreation (designed by landscape architect Michelle Devine), has been absorbed into our proposals by employing fingers of green space between buildings.

Within the housing areas, courtyard spaces constructed over podium garages reinvent the London square. These spaces, landscaped as an ecological resource as well as an amenity for human occupants, are controlled by the residents who live around them. Thus the physical infrastructure will include a range of private, semi-private and shared public spaces. The school and health centre complex (designed by Edward Cullinan Architects) will provide an important community focus and add to the sense of mixed use development.

The physical masterplan is of fundamental importance to creating a sense of place, but you cannot divorce 'place making' from the issue of how it is managed. Our competition entry postulated a process by which residents will not only be able to participate in community development but also be stakeholders involved in the long term management of the Village. A Village Trust will be established which will be endowed with funds from the development process and receive revenue income. Information

Case studies

9.6 *Same block in 2005 (a), 2007 (b) and 2015 (c). Flexibility and organic growth are key concepts at the Greenwich Millennium Village. Architects: HTA and Ralph Erskine*

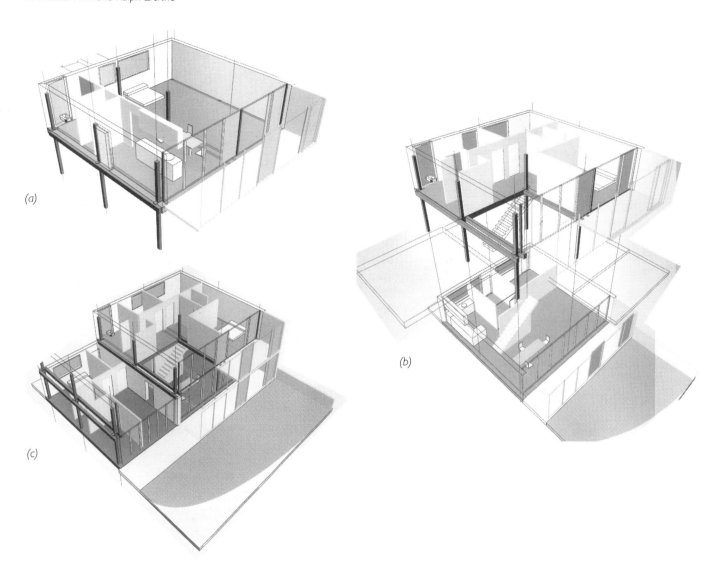

(a)

(b)

(c)

technology will play a central role in this process as well as assisting in economic regeneration by giving people access to training and jobs. The idea is to establish a Village web site so that people can trade in services at a local level. The IT infrastructure could, at little further cost, also be extended to create links with management, environmental control and security.

Our entry attempted a very broad response to the issues that confront us in revitalising cities, tackling social exclusion, developing brownfield sites, innovating in con-

struction and improving choice in housing. This wide range of measures have a common purpose – to create sustainable places where people want to live. Place making needs to embrace all of these issues if we are to reverse the trend towards depopulation of our city centres. Our ambition at Greenwich is to make a new kind of urban place that will meet all the aspirations of people who would otherwise go to the suburbs. This is the challenge of sustainable housing: to make the inner city sufficiently attractive to reverse the presumption in favour of greenfield development.

9.7 *Interior views of typical apartment: from balcony (top), and living area (bottom). Notice the flexible planning with sliding or folding screens.*
Architects: HTA and Ralph Erskine

10

Sustainable housing in Manchester: a case study of Hulme

GEORGE MILLS

The 19th century plan of Hulme illustrates the benefits of a dense urban network of streets in a grid iron pattern. The layout supported a wide range of human activity: living, shopping, education, employment and all the elements of urban life that constitute working neighbourhoods. It was a classic example of what we are now beginning to refer to as a sustainable urban village. Within a 5 to 10 minute walk of any dwelling most of the facilities necessary for the sustenance of an urban settlement were to be found. In many ways Hulme 100 years ago was the essence of a sustainable community.

The area was not identifiable as a particular estate or neighbourhood; it took its place in the urban matrix of Manchester as an inner city neighbourhood. As a physical infrastructure it promoted a high degree of social and economic activity, not the segregation that is the major characteristic of post war planning. Sadly the area was destroyed when Hulme underwent major change in the 1950s and 1960s. At its zenith in 1900, 130,000 people lived in Hulme, but as a consequence of changing patterns of employment and industry, planning and migration, over the past 30 years this population has been reduced to 25,000 people.

During the 1950s and 1960s the whole area, save for a handful of pubs and churches, was razed to the ground under Manchester City Council's slum clearance programme. Hulme was redeveloped in the form of five large estates, physically identified by differing prefabricated building systems, and severed from the rest of the city by elevated and subterranean pedestrian routes, and sunken arterial road systems. Central to the area's redevelopment were the notorious 'Crescents', four deck access, sweeping, concrete mega-structures, all ironically named after famous 18th and 19th century architects.

10.1 *Plan of Hulme (top), Manchester in c1880.*

10.2 *Aerial view of the centre of Hulme (bottom) in the 1960s, showing the four Crescents.*

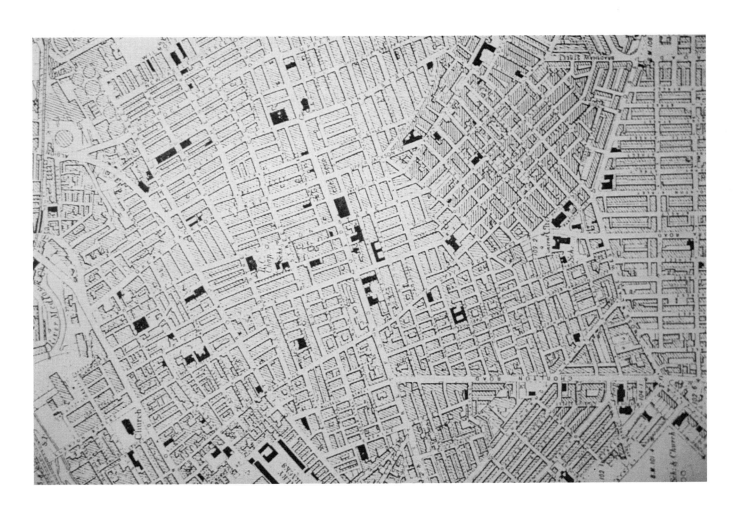

Case studies

10.3 *Barrie Crescent, Hulme undergoing demolition. This example is typical of the balcony access, system built blocks.*

10.4 *MBLC masterplan (1991) for the urban restructuring of Hulme.*

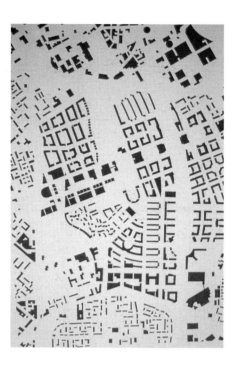

The image that the area projected as a consequence of the redevelopment was of large scaled new buildings generally of high density and mainly high rise in construction. The reality, however, was that in Hulme's redevelopment the population had shrunk by 75% to the point where the number of people living and working in the area was so low that even the most basic services and amenities could not be supported. The density of housing had fallen from that of the Victorian terraces (approximately 60 dwellings to the acre), to suburban levels (14 dwellings to the acre) by the predominantly deck access system of redevelopment.

Management of the Crescents proved extremely difficult and within a few years the original families who had been allocated to them were being rehoused elsewhere in the city, and from the mid-1970s onwards the blocks were inhabited by a mixture of students, ex-students and other social groups with very limited economic potential. As a consequence Hulme became isolated from the vibrancy, economy and culture of the City at large and people living in the area were increasingly disenfranchised.

In terms of a basically sustainable neighbourhood, Hulme had failed and a solution to the physical, environmental and economic problems of the area was sought by the City Council. The government's announcement in 1991 of the City Challenge Initiative provided an ideal vehicle for the council to promote Hulme as an area for yet further regeneration. Using the £37.5 million on offer to the winners of the City Challenge bids, the council planned to clear away the deck access blocks and rebuild Hulme as an integrated living and working neighbourhood.

The proposals for the regeneration of Hulme were accepted and the programme for the demolition and reconstruction of the area began in 1992. A key element of the reconstruction was the provision of housing types across a broad economic spectrum and a fundamental change in the management, ownership and tenure of residential accommodation within the area. High on the agenda was addressing the low number of people living in the area and the planning strategy on redevelopment was the achievement of a minimum density of 30–35 dwellings to the acre. A conceptual masterplan was prepared by Mills,

10.5 *Figure ground comparisons: Victorian Hulme (left); deck-access blocks, 1960 (middle); MBLC masterplan, 1993 (bottom).*

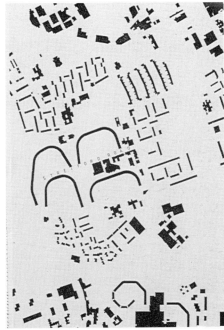
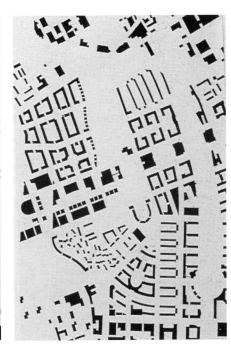

Beaumont, Leavey and Channon (MBLC) Architects supported by a design code to underpin the principles on which Hulme was to be rebuilt.

The Hulme Design Guide, based on the original code and influenced by work in America by architects Duaney/Plater Zyberk, was adopted by the City Council in 1993. The technical guidance within the Design Guide challenged many of the codes of practice and planning legislation that had governed post war development in English cities. MBLC was employed by the City Council to implement the guidance and ensure that all new development in Hulme achieved acceptable standards of urban design.

The Hulme Design Guide was purposely prescriptive. This was felt necessary as low density, inward looking, suburban based development was beginning to proliferate around the city centre. Such development does little for the promotion of vibrant public places, creating instead privatised, enclosed and introverted developments of low density, limited variety and short term value.

Simple rules with respect to hierarchy, permeability and integration are translated in the Design Guide into strategies and technical dimensions for defining how streets, open spaces and urban blocks are to be formed, creating a framework within which different architects and developers can work collaboratively. Allied to the guidance is the aim of achieving a balanced community with a mix of tenures including an initial 1,000 social housing units to be developed by The Guinness Trust and North British Housing Association, and 1,000 private sector houses and flats for sale or rent with associated retail/commercial and social facilities.

The intention in Hulme is to completely reverse the area's decline and recreate an economically and socially diverse neighbourhood, less vulnerable to changes in the city's fortunes. As masterplan architects the diversity and variety of what is built is of primary concern to ourselves. In implementing the Design Guide we were at pains to avoid dictating the style or materials used for new buildings. Our first concern was with the footprint of new development, how buildings related to one another, and how they integrated themselves into the overall framework of this part of the city.

10.6 *Redevelopment in progress following MBLC Design Guide. Notice the re-establishment of 'streets'.*

To date, some 13 different firms of architects have been involved in the redevelopment of Hulme. Collectively they have produced designs that may not in some instances be of the highest architectural quality, but they represent the ethos of variety, which given Hulme's recent past, is absolutely essential. If Hulme teaches us anything it is the desirability of employing a number of practices working to a design guide rather than allowing a single architect to impose a solution throughout. One of Hulme's major problems was, and to a certain extent still is, the stigma, reputation and notoriety created in the minds of people by a dominant style, manner and scale of architecture.

'Homes for Change' and 'Work for Change' buildings

It has proved difficult to overcome the stigma attached to the term 'deck access' which within Manchester at least, is seen as a manifestation of all that is bad in modern urban housing. As a practice MBLC was employed in 1992 by two co-operatives, Homes for Change (HFC) and Work for Change (WFC) to design a high density, mixed use urban building as part of the regeneration of Hulme. All of the people involved in the scheme had lived in the former deck access blocks and were aware of the shortcomings and advantages of the system as a residential building form.

In order to achieve comparable densities to those found in European cities, housing schemes need to embrace strategies that go beyond limited variants of two storey terraced and semi-detached formats. The HFC building is essentially a courtyard formed by four, five and six storey wings connected by access decks and roof gardens. Within the building there are 50 dwellings, work space, office accommodation, a theatre, cafe, restaurant and studios. The dwellings vary from one bedroom gallery flats to four bedroom apartments. This variation means that people whose social circumstances change are not forced into leaving the building and living elsewhere, they can simply move to larger or smaller accommodation within the basic structure. An important factor within this scheme is the density, equating to something like 120 dwellings to the acre and hence about twice the Victorian density.

In many ways the HFC building epitomises the lifestyle, culture and diversity of the former Crescents. This is a consequence of the collaboration between architects and users, and the dynamic chemistry that results from true participation in design. The building stems from a productive dialogue between The Guinness Trust, the HFC and WFC Co-operatives, design team, and a local authority that understood the need to ensure that responsive yet contemporary architecture had a place in the future of Hulme. It is ironic that Le Corbusier's Unite d'Habitation in Marseilles proved a reference and precedent for the HFC building yet his ideas are often blamed for all that is bad in modern urban housing. His philosophy, however, with regard to the requisite components of good urban architecture forms the basis for this building.

The importance of the Masterplan

The Hulme Masterplan and Design Guide seeks innovation in the housing provided by both public and private sectors. The development of flats and houses that successfully turn and define the corner, for example, though common in more densely populated European cities, is an art the guide seeks to revive. Having become accustomed to designing isolated freestanding buildings (primarily as a consequence of zoning policies) British architects have had to address this simple urban block afresh.

A significant contributor to the revitalised urban nature of Hulme is the reduction in the local authority's requirements for car parking. Had the previous legislation been adhered to, 43 of the 250 acres of Hulme would have been taken up with surface parking. The use of on-street parking and the overall reduction from 100% requirements to somewhere in the region of 50% means that the car no longer dominates the public realm.

It is encouraging that as the regeneration of Hulme progressed after 1992, the quality of design and development improved. Public authorities began to understand the basic nature of the Hulme Design Guide, and for many architects who feared initially that it would be a restrictive

Case studies

Table 10.1 Key elements of design guide for Hulme, Manchester

Streets
—   buildings should front onto streets
—   streets are for walking
—   should be 'eyes' to the street
—   doors on to streets should be at no more than 15m intervals
—   residential ground floors should be 450mm above pavement level

Integration
—   housing should not look like 'estates'
—   all uses accommodated within an integrated pattern of streets
—   streets should contain a variety of uses
—   space should be left to accommodate later uses

Density
—   housing should average 90 units/hectare
—   development should be along main routes and focal points first and this should be at the highest density

Permeability
—   all streets should lead to other streets
—   streets should encourage through movement
—   there should be a variety of routes available
—   the grain of streets should be finer around modes of activity

Routes and transport
—   public transport should be planned as an integral part of the street layout
—   street design should reduce vehicle speed rather than ease traffic flow
—   on-street parking is encouraged
—   the impact of the car should be minimised
—   the abuse of on-street parking must be avoided
—   in-curtilage parking should be avoided in front of houses
—   traditional crossroads are encouraged
—   safe routes for cyclists should be provided

Landmarks, vistas and focal points
—   development should optimise existing vistas and create new ones
—   corner buildings should consolidate the urban composition
—   major street junctions should be designed as 'places'
—   civic and community buildings should be located around public spaces
—   existing landmarks should be incorporated into the urban structure
—   buildings of under 100m^2 can be of any height
—   public art should give character to urban spaces

(contd)

Table 10.1 (contd)

Definition of space
– building lines should create unbroken urban edges
– where buildings are set back from the street, they should have a public presence
– there should be a clear definition between public and private space
– street, squares and parks should be clearly defined by appropriately scaled buildings and trees
– building elevations should be scaled to the proportions of the street

Identity
– existing buildings should be enhanced to avoid the feeling that everything is the same age
– large buildings should not distort the scale of streets
– buildings should respond to location
– different materials and finishes are encouraged
– diversity of design solutions is encouraged

Sustainability
– design for change of use is encouraged
– new buildings should be designed for low maintenance
– existing trees should be retained and new street trees provided
– maintenance burdens of open space should be considered
– urban nature conservation measures should be considered
– space for segregate waste storage should be provided
– all new housing should attain 'good' on the BREDEM scale
– new homes should achieve at least level 8 on the National Energy Rating

Hierarchy
– the scale of buildings should reflect the hierarchy and urban character of different types of streets

Source: Adapted from The Design Guide for Hulme, 1998

Table 10.2 Key technical requirements for regeneration of Hulme, Manchester

	High streets	*Secondary streets*	*Residential streets*
Recommended distance between building lines	21m max	17.5m max	15.5m max
Number of building storeys	4-6	3-5	2-3
Percentage of frontages complying with enclosure rates	90%	80%	60%
Carriageway width	10m max	7m	6m
Footpath width	2.5m max	1.8m	1.8m
Additional margin for street trees	1.2m	1.2m	1.2m
Cycle lane	2m	2m	within carriageway
Speed limit	30mph	30mph	20mph
Kerb radii	10m	6m	3m

Source: Adapted from The Design Guide for Hulme, 1998

10.9 *'Homes for Change' building designed by MBLC, general view.*

10.10 *'Homes for Change', building detail (opposite).*
Architect: MBLC

Table 10.3 Guidelines for enclosure ratio of different types of urban space at Hulme, Manchester

---

Streets Height to width between 1:1.5 and 1:2.5

Squares Height to width between 1:4 and 1:5

Parks   Height to width between 1:7 and 1:10

Source: Adapted from The Design Guide for Hulme, 1998

straightjacket, it proved helpful. It was described by a developer recently as 'a tool for liberating the talented designer but also for controlling the poor one'. Irrespective of whether housing is privately or publicly funded, the variety and distinction within each development illustrates that identity can be given to individual buildings whilst allowing the whole to be part of a family of structures.

It is the addition of significant numbers of private dwellings to the existing public stock that has been the key to Hulme's renewed life. Dwellings that initially sold for under £30,000 are now changing hands at nearly £40,000. Developers who were originally sceptical about the prospects for the area are now building a variety of accommodation including maisonettes, three storey dwellings and gallery access flats.

To claim that the current regeneration of Hulme has worked would be premature but the mixture and diversity that makes urban neighbourhoods sustainable is already present. Although the rebuilding of Hulme began in the economic recession of the early 1990s, enough critical mass of buildings exists to be optimistic about the future. Each subsequent development that takes place tends to be of higher density and better quality than previous projects. The construction of social, commercial and retail properties is also beginning to complement the residential re-development that was the initial ambition behind the City Challenge process. As local businesses begin to view Hulme as having changed beyond recognition, it is hoped that the area will once again function with the economic and social vibrancy of former times. Sustainability at Hulme has been the result of partnership, a commitment to social cohesion through strong urban design, and the promotion of variety within spatial order.

11

A personal vision of sustainable housing

EDWARD CULLINAN

Aspect, territory and shelter

If you imagine how they built houses in London in the 18th century, you will realise that they dug big basements from street through to mews, they then raised the level of street and mews by dumping rubbish from the basement on them. As a result they were often left with clay for making bricks with. Sometimes the house must have risen directly out of the same hole its bricks came from. One day, when we have thought up the right handling systems, we might do it again.

The house we built for ourselves in the early 1960s (see Figure 11.1) is made of heavy, mass materials from which light materials hang. The heavy materials are concrete and second hand London Stock bricks which rise solid, thick and carved from the London clay upon which they sit, to make party walls or territorial boundaries on either side of the site. Also heavy is a line of concrete columns down the middle of the site, and on the south side, a garage/workshop with steps that mount up and over it to be the front steps to the first floor of the house. Thus the heavy ground is coaxed up to become a seat for the house (Figure 11.2).

Upon this seat are hung the light materials, sticks to start with, then plywood, then glass. A wooden beam rests across the concrete columns, roof joists and floor joists span from on top of it to the ledged party wall. Windows and cupboards are dangled down from the joist ends, overhanging at every joint and open jointed, all in 'deal', or technically Swedish 5th Whitewood.

Most rainstorms in London are fairly vertical, so by overhanging like this you move the house in a southerly direction to somewhere like Florence, which makes it last longer and work better. The overhangs also make for solar shading on the south side of the house, aided by a tree in

11.1 *Ted Cullinan House,
London in c1965.*

the summer. The words had not been invented then, but it is a 'passive solar house'.

The typical section contains 'closed plan' bedrooms in the 'heavy' downstairs and an open plan gallery living space encased by lightweight sticks above. The typicality of the section is broken only near the middle, where two joists project to engage on the front steps, to invite entry.

The house, put together out of pieces of unshaped 75 × 75 and 75 × 150 softwood and 6 mm Douglas Fir ply

has lasted beautifully for 35 years; only one piece of softwood, a sill with an exposed top surface, has rotted in all those years. The pieces of wood are never housed into one another, they are cross jointed and bolted with timber connectors, and the section ensures that they always drip clear of one another; softwood looks after itself if it is allowed to dry out frequently enough.

Although described from a practical point of view, the house that creates and frames its own territory, both inside

Case studies

11.2 *Sequence of construction of Ted Cullinan House, London 1962-66 (6 views).*

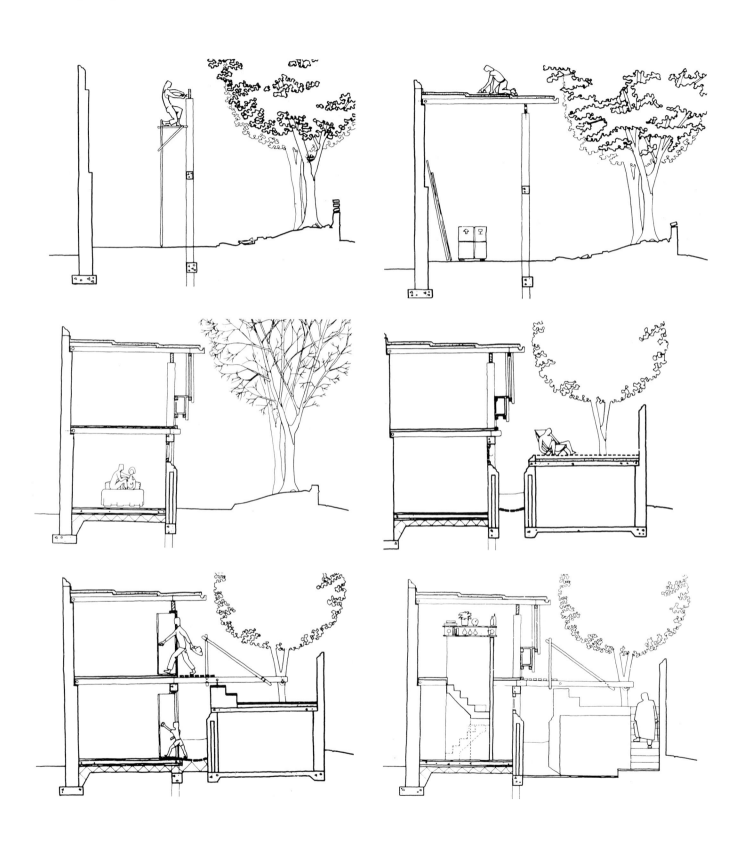

11.3 *House in Zanzibar constructed of thin lengths of greenwood.*

and out, is above all a piece of modern architecture. It is inspired by the de Stijl tradition: pieces dropped on top of one another, offered up against one another, and the spaces being imagined as the space or place bounded by the sticks.

Of course, the roof went on first to create a secure, waterproof site between weekend building sessions, then the rest was built downwards beneath it. Eventually, it was habitable, we moved in, continued to finish it for a few more years and we have lived there ever since.

Conservation and the use of resources

The picture of the house being built in Zanzibar (Figure 11.3) from amazingly thin pieces of greenwood, like a basket, is to introduce the next house that I want to describe. I am quite envious about the economy of means of the Zanzibar house.

We have in Britain acres and acres of forest thinnings that are usually burnt, often pulped or dumped on landfill sites, sometimes made into fence posts or Sterling Board. John Makepeace was interested in using these forest thinnings to make buildings.

In some ways, it is the opposite of going into a forest and cutting down big trees to make log cabins or to make cabers to toss in competition! It is more like trying to use all the pieces found for their most useful purpose, as in the Japanese tradition, or making bows and arrows that shoot by using tension and bending. It is about cutting down long thin pieces of greenwood which have to be cut down, treated and used quickly. Used within a day they bend further and more easily than they do after a week, and so on. A simple diagram consists of two long poles, tied together at the top, then pushed in and locked into the foundations; basically what Richard Burton, Frei Otto and Ted Happold did earlier when they built a wood making factory in the same forest in Dorset – Hooke Park.

The house illustrated is one of five proposed. It is an extremely simple house, based on the notion of the holiday house where unlike more conventional houses, there is no distinction between public and private space. It is in fact a study house, with eight bedrooms and bathrooms, planned around a large central living space. The system of making this house basically consists of getting long thin pieces of wood, lashing them together and resting them across the bathrooms which act as trestles; then pulling them down across the rest of the house to form a lattice. With bentwood construction you want continuous curves which are set up by the bent wood itself. Then, the convex corners are webbed, which acts rather like cross bracing, so you have a great big bentwood umbrella over both the private places around the edge and the shared space in the middle.

Case studies

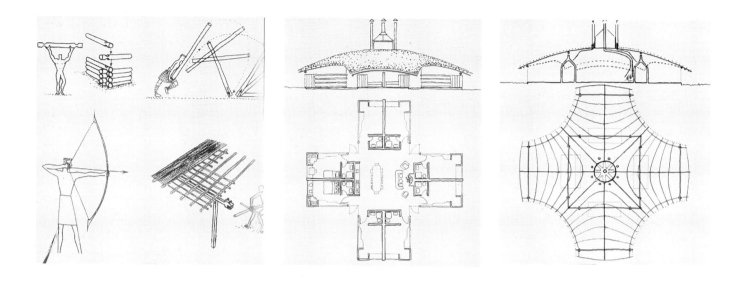

11.4 *Concept drawings and model of John Makepeace House, Hooke Park, Dorset.*

11.5 View of completed John Makepeace House in forest setting complete with turf roof.

The whole umbrella is then covered with a greenwood planked deck, insulation and turf; the stability of the whole depends on the linear fibrous strength of bendy greenwood.

There will be other, more sophisticated houses on the site, exploring 'solar gain' design and the use of recycled materials.

Heaviness and insulation at Greenwich

Last year, we contributed to the Osborne, Manhattan Loft, Peabody entry for the Greenwich Millennium Village Competition. There was a beefy masterplan by Piers Gough, allowing the prongs of a new, riverside park to pierce through into the shared gardens of housing schemes; fenced shared gardens, Kensington style. Robust it needed to be, since there were 12 architects involved, including Foster, Hopkins, Hadid and Coates.

Thickness, heaviness, aspect, and a very high level of insulation, were the basic means of achieving sustainability in our various schemes for houses, flats, duplexes, offices, shops, cinema, underground parking, play areas and leisure gardens. We were also interested in how to make a continuous edge to the shared space which would also read as a series of separate apartment buildings.

This was achieved by devising the service core plans shown in the picture; a lift/stair core around which one, two, three, four and five bedroom flats, studios, duplexes and triplexes are grouped, shedding and gathering bedrooms, one from another. Plenty of balconies exist in the

11.6 *Model of Greenwich
Millennium Village proposal.*

convex spaces, where one stair/lift tower melts into its neighbour, and as the buildings diminish toward the top. Where towers stop short of the 12 floor maximum, there are full scale gardens on the roof. There are family houses too, and the whole project is for sale and rent mixed up.

I began by talking about sustainability in the sense of making territory, building construction, solar gain and sheltering from the rain, which I think are all things we definitely have to find an aesthetic to do elegantly. I also suggested that some of the early traditions of the modern movement might inspire us when responding to these new demands. I then moved to the use of material, which would otherwise be thrown away, and then on to how to make dense urban schemes through using thickness, heaviness and insulation at macro and micro level.

11.7 *Plans and elevations of proposal for Greenwich Millennium Village.*

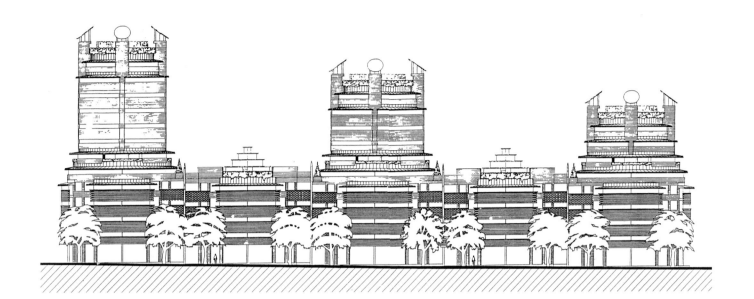

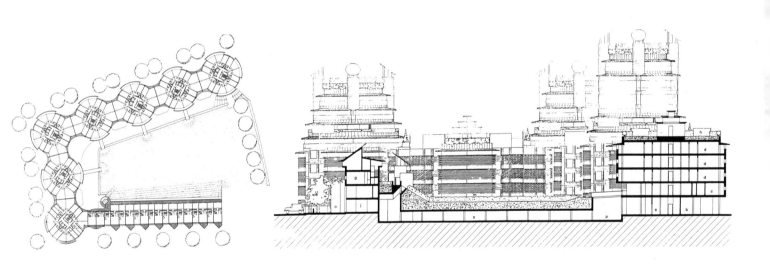

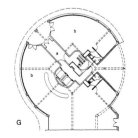
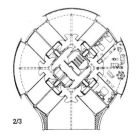

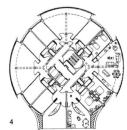
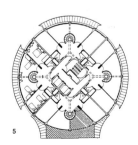

Case studies

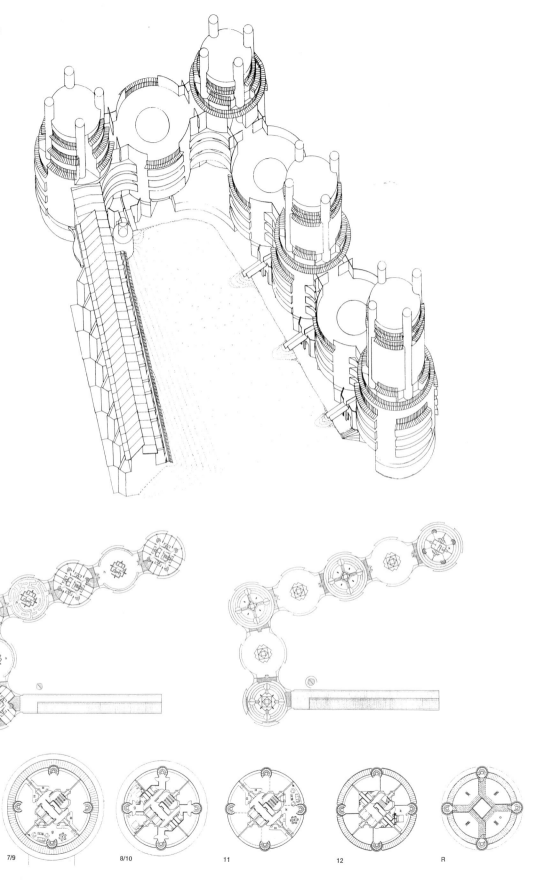

11.8 *The interlocking of blocks in the Greenwich Millennium Village project.*

6   7/9   8/10   11   12   R

The future

12

Towards sustainable housing: principles and practice

DAVID TURRENT

It is perhaps worthwhile reminding readers of the background to the current preoccupation with sustainable development. The key points to remember are:

- Global warming is now an accepted scientific fact. Average annual temperatures are likely to rise by 1.5°C over the next 50 years. Many parts of the UK, particularly the east coast will be prone to flooding as sea levels rise.
- Acid rain is also a problem. Over 20% of Britain's trees are affected, according to the Forestry Commission.
- Rainforest destruction is continuing despite the efforts of environmental campaigners resulting in a 15% contribution to greenhouse gas emissions. It is still difficult in practice to trace the source of timber used in the building industry, in spite of recent Kite schemes.
- Air quality in urban areas is a major problem with consequent cost to the health service. Asthma in young children is the fastest growing illness in the late 1990s.
- The ozone hole is getting bigger, now extending to large areas over Antarctica, with a smaller but growing area over the Arctic. As the ozone layer thins, extra ultra violet radiation reaches the Earth's surface leading to an increase in skin cancer and eye cataracts.
- We know that buildings contribute a significant proportion of the CO_2 emissions which are a major cause of global warming. In fact about 50% of all emissions in the UK are the result of heating, lighting and ventilating buildings.

12.1 *ECD designed housing in Hulme, Manchester.*

Architects and environmental ethics

As architects we have a special responsibility to make our buildings as efficient and robust as possible. The rate of demolition of the existing housing stock has slowed down over the past decade with the result that the typical house today will probably outlive its design life by a factor of three. In fact, recent research suggests that the life of a typical English house is above 100 years.

The drive towards sustainability requires a new approach to housing design. There is a complex set of issues that requires an integrated, holistic approach from the micro to the macro scale and greater co-operation between design-

ers, procurers and users. This may involve architects advising their clients on the selection of a site through to advice on how to run and maintain buildings after occupation.

The cradle to grave approach is the basis of sustainability with materials chosen for their robustness in use and minimum adverse impact on the environment. In design terms we need a framework within which to set targets and make decisions. My own practice has found the following useful pointers to consider.

Energy

Reduced dependence on fossil fuel use lies at the heart of sustainable design. Energy efficiency in new housing

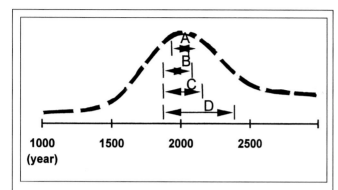

'A' life of commercial building (50 years)

'B' lifespan of domestic building (100 years)

'C' lifespan of public building (200 years)

'D' lifespan of infrastructure (400 years)

can be improved significantly beyond the requirements of current Building Regulations at no great additional cost. A wide range of technical information is available, specifically through the Best Practice Guides published by BRECSU.

- Energy targets can be set using either SAP or NHER ratings. CO_2 targets may also be introduced in the future
- where possible housing layouts should be designed to take maximum advantage of passive solar heat gain
- compact built forms with low wall/floor ratios are more efficient in terms of reducing heat loss
- a thermal insulation standard of 0.3 Wm²K in walls and floors and 0.25 Wm²K in roofs is cost effective and quite easily achieved
- super-insulation standards of 0.1–0.2 Wm²K can be achieved technically especially in non-traditional construction
- electricity consumption represents a rising proportion of the domestic annual fuel bill. Low energy lights and energy efficient white goods should be specified where possible
- solar water heating systems have a lengthy payback

period in the UK but are worth considering as part of a package of measures aimed at reducing CO_2 (subscript) emissions
- photovoltaic installations have payback periods of 50–100 years currently but are likely to be more widely used in the future as prices drop and cell efficiency improves.

Materials

Greater care needs to be taken in the specification of building materials, with a preference for locally sourced materials where possible. This is particularly true of heavy bulky materials where energy transport costs can be significant.

- An embodied energy audit can provide useful guidelines for consideration at the design stage
- consideration should be given to the use of recycled materials e.g. timber, bricks, roofing tiles
- cellulose insulation made from recycled newsprint can be used safely in timber frame construction
- new components such as masonite beams offer a high strength to weight ratio and make use of recycled timber
- prefabricated or factory made components reduce the amount of waste generated and minimise dust contamination on site
- natural materials such as timber, stone and linoleum should be used in preference to polymer based products.

Water

Water will become an increasingly valuable resource as the number of households increases and demand threatens to outstrip supply. Designers can do much to reduce domestic water consumption, by as much as one third, with relatively simple measures.

- Specification of low flush or dual flush WCs
- use of flow restrictors and spray taps
- collection of rainwater for garden irrigation

- recycling of grey water for use in flushing WCs. Commercial systems are now coming on the market
- where space is available use of reed beds for cleaning rainwater or even treating solid waste
- design of permeable surfaces externally to reduce run-off
- use of water meters to raise awareness of water consumption.

Transport

The location of housing close to public transport interchanges is central to the concept of sustainable development. Ideally every dwelling should be within 400m of a public transport facility.

- The aim of sustainable development is not necessarily to eliminate the car but to reduce car use
- by the same token housing layouts should be designed to give priority to pedestrians and cyclists
- consideration needs to be given to provision of secure cycle storage in or adjacent to the dwelling
- a local IT infrastructure can be a useful aid in facilitating car pooling
- mixed use neighbourhoods reduce the demand made upon car transport.

The future

12.4 *Four examples of low energy housing at Energy World, Milton Keynes, 1988. Each maximises solar gain using the building fabric as a heat store.*

12.5 *Linacre College, Oxford designed to explore sustainable construction using local materials and low energy design. ECD Architects*

Table 12.1 UK government's four objectives of sustainable development and the consequences for the construction industry

Social progress that meets needs of everyone	–	emphasis upon sustainable housing
	–	access through education
	–	improved public transport
Effective protection of the environment	–	stricter measures on water extraction
	–	new planning guidelines to protect green belts
	–	stricter waste and pollution policies
Prudent use of natural resources	–	higher energy standards
	–	new water conservation measures
	–	additional controls on quarrying
High and stable levels of economic growth	–	enhancing educational performance
	–	improving access to training
	–	providing infrastructure for business growth

Source: Adapted from UK Strategy for Sustainable Development, 1996

Table 12.2 Key targets for carbon dioxide (CO_2) reduction

- UK government commitment to stabilise increase in CO_2 by 2000
- UK government voluntary target of 20% reduction in CO_2 by 2010 (compared with 1990 levels)
- EU commitment to reduce CO_2 by 8% (over 1990 levels) by 2010

Quality of life

Sustainability is not just about physical issues, it embraces a whole range of social, aesthetic and economic concerns relating to the well-being of the individual and the community:

- Indoor and outside air quality is an important issue in reducing ill health

12.6 *Greenwich Millennium Village proposals by ECD Architects using prefabricated construction.*

12.7 *Experimental eco-houses built at Stuttgart Garden Festival in 1993 with double height, south facing winter gardens (opposite). Architect: ECD Architects*

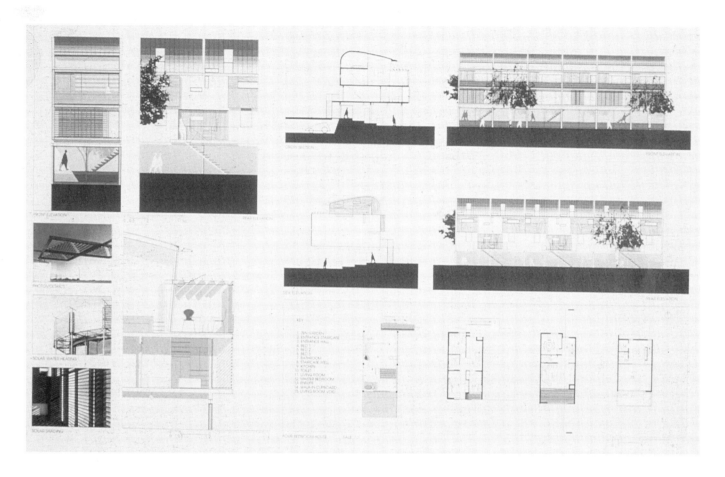

- VOCs (volatile organic compounds) are released by solvent based preservatives
- landscape needs to be integrated with housing and wildlife encouraged
- users need to be involved in the process of design and management of their estates.

Conclusion

Architects can do much to help achieve sustainable housing by using their design skills to create higher density, mixed use neighbourhoods utilising smaller urban sites than normally considered viable by volume house builders. In the process, energy, water and material use can be reduced by applying specific not standard solutions to housing problems. The picture presented by sustainable development is complex and many types of solution are possible depending upon the priorities or conditions of a particular site. Green housing is not easy to achieve, especially within the constraints of typical housing budgets, but when over a quarter of all CO_2 emissions are the result of how we heat, light and ventilate dwellings, there is no alternative approach to housing design.

13

Design guidelines for sustainable housing

BRIAN EDWARDS

The attainment of sustainable housing is a growing ambition for all in the construction industry. No society is balanced and sustainable unless housing addresses difficult issues such as social exclusion, crime and employment opportunities as well as the usual priorities of energy and environmental performance. Along with job security and education, housing is central to the public's perception of quality of life. However, since housing is multi-faceted, the attainment of sustainable housing requires teamwork between the professions in the construction industry. Collaboration between architects and planners, between the public and private sectors, between users and providers, designers and contractors is essential if sustainable housing is to become a reality.

Sustainable housing is a matter of both the design and management of the housing stock. A decent home of whatever type is central to social cohesion, personal well-being and the creation of successful communities. Whereas sustainable development balances economic growth with environmental capacity, the task of building sustainable communities involves finding ways of integrating social, economic and environmental goals. Communities of the future will need to live more in equilibrium with nature than in the past. This requires rethinking how we design buildings, how we lay out estates, how towns connect with their surroundings and interrelate with natural resources. Action is required of us all – government, professions, industry, communities and individuals.

Lifestyle change cannot be imposed but it can be encouraged by good design. It is relatively easy to evolve new ideas but too often in the construction industry old ideas get in the way of implementing fresh thinking. Design holds the key to unlocking future potential and to

13.1 *Low energy village at Lund, Sweden designed by Krister Wiberg (general view (top) and detail (bottom)).*

Table 13.1 Some key definitions of sustainability

— Sustainable development
"Development that meets the needs of the present without compromising the ability of future generations to meet their own needs."
(Brundtland, 1987)
— Sustainable design
"Creating buildings which are energy efficient, healthy, comfortable, flexible in use and designed for long life."
(Foster and Partners, 1999)
— Sustainable construction
"The creation and management of healthy buildings based upon resource efficient and ecological principles."
(BSRIA, Centre for Construction Ecology, 1996)

presenting new ideas in a way that breaks down barriers to change. There is no future for sustainable housing without a culture change in society.

The DETR report *Building a Sustainable Future: Homes for an Autonomous Community*, reviews some of the issues involved in sustainable housing.[1] It argues that sustainable communities might include measures such as:

- local generation of energy using renewable sources such as wind, solar and biomass
- the interconnection of work, housing, community and leisure facilities
- the provision of opportunities for local employment
- new housing design compatible with more sustainable lifestyles.

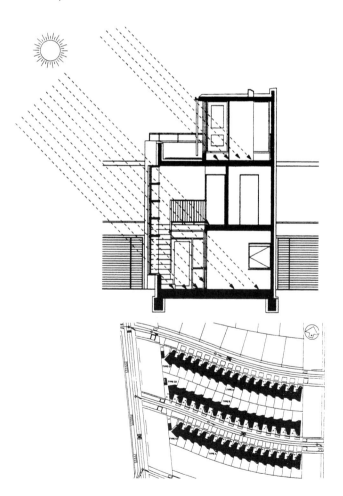

These measures have the potential to provide stable, self reliant communities. As for the houses, the report suggests that these are likely to be super-insulated, of high thermal mass, airtight in construction and made from building materials based upon non toxic, low embodied energy principles. In addition, the sustainable house will (just as in the co-authors' Robert and Brenda Vale's own house) feature water collection from the rain, sewage treatment on site using reedbeds and composting techniques, waste recycling and local energy generation.

The sustainable housing estate

The sustainable house is dependent upon integrated design and this is equally true of sustainable communities where the principles underpinning the individual house are multiplied several times over. At the level of the housing estate, questions of land use policy, density of development, integration of transport, social mix, ownership and tenure mix, all become important. Decisions made at the planning level will inevitably affect construction decisions.

One thing is certain of sustainability and that is that lifestyles will need to change. At first, change will be by persuasion, but later compulsion may be needed. Ultimately legislation will be the motor of lifestyle change. At the masterplanning level lifestyles will need to adapt to denser layouts, less land use segregation, more social interaction, less private transport access and very much altered housing design. For instance, the maximising of passive solar gain will result in a preference for southern orientation of dwellings with houses looking different on opposite sides of the road (Figures 13.1 and 13.2). Blocks may be more widely spaced (for solar aperture) but higher and denser in layout. Since heat loss is critical, future housing will use terraced and flatted forms as against detached and semi-detached.

Housing layout too will incorporate measures to improve the microclimate. Courtyard layout may be preferred - possibly using south facing courts – with dense tree planting providing shelter at the edge of estates or summertime shading near to houses. Places exposed, such as the periphery of the estate or rooftops, will probably exploit passive energy sources such as the wind and sun.

Housing of the future will not be functionally separate

13.3 *Low energy housing in Stornoway, Scotland, designed in 1985 by Technical Services Department of Western Isles Island Council. Single storey adaptable house (top); two storey terraced house with shared sun space (bottom).*

plan : 3 person house

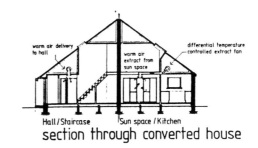

section through converted house

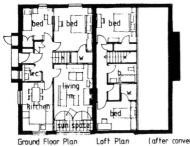

plans : 3-6 person convertible

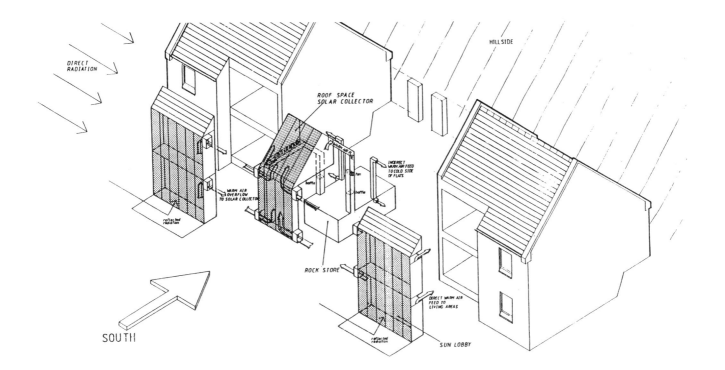

The future

13.4 *Culture change for a green future.*

13.5 *New building in Temple Bar, Dublin which exploits various sources of renewable energy – wind, solar and geothermal. Architect: Murray O'Laoire*

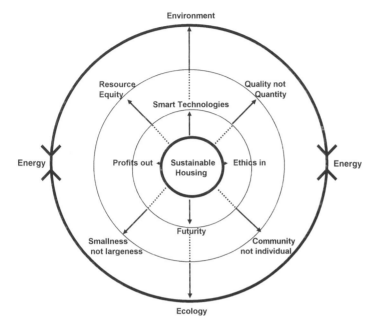

Table 13.2 Sustainable housing estate planning

- concentrate development in mixed use neighbourhoods
- use terraced or flatted solutions
- exploit CHP opportunities
- use development clusters related to public transport
- integrate with cycle or walking routes
- exploit solar layouts
- provide shelter
- integrate energy estate planning with safe streets policies
- ensure mixed use and mixed tenure
- exploit aesthetic potential of high density

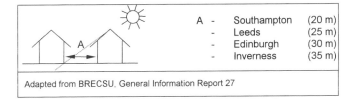

and isolated as in the past but constructed within neighbourhoods or blocks containing other land uses. The close integration of different functions into overlapping zones of activity will drastically alter the face of housing. Existing residential neighbourhoods will come under pressure to absorb other land uses within garden space or lofts whilst new housing areas will not be monocultures as in the past. The change opens up opportunities for innovative design with the emphasis upon the small builder not large contractor, and on site specific not universal solutions.

Since passive solar gains can make an important contribution to reducing energy consumption in housing (by as much as 18% without house type change) orientation of dwellings should be up to 30° either side of south.[2] Coupled with this the area of glazing should be restricted to the north and enlarged to the south. As glazing areas are partly a function of room needs, this results in houses of differential layout according to aspect. A delicate balance, however, has to be struck between solar gain, heat loss, daylight need, and double or triple glazing. Also the fabric should be able to absorb and store the passive gains by incorporating high thermal mass (Figure 13.3).

Site layout for maximising solar gain has implications for plan and section. To achieve solar penetration between houses an unobstructed angle of 10° is needed on south elevations. This is particularly true where roof mounted photovoltaic panels are used. Housing layout with a preference for a southerly aspect requires care in planting design to avoid reducing the solar benefits by poor landscape design and to create shelter. Wind tunnels are the result of parallel alignments and in residential areas – particularly in northern locations – windbreaks are needed. The general rule is to create perimeter shelter for the neighbourhood using a mixture of coniferous and deciduous planting, and to use specimen trees closer to the house. The best choices are open foliage species (such as ash or rowan) which shed their leaves in winter when solar gains are most needed.

Into these planted corridors the network of cycle and walkways are best placed. Windbreaks are helpful in reducing the surface exposure or speed of air movement around dwellings, but they also provide attractive areas for recreation or local wildlife. Such areas can also be used to absorb rainwater (especially when paving is porous), for community waste or composting schemes, and to help provide biodiversity at the site. Where reedbed water purification is employed, these areas can also be incorporated into shelter belts. Site layout needs not only to facilitate green principles but to gesture towards the desirability of more sustainable lifestyles. This is particularly true with non-car based transport. Urban design should make car journeys difficult and frustrating at the level of the residential estate in order to reduce the 29% of CO_2 emissions nationally that are the result of transportation.

Since trains are the gateway to a sustainable future, modern high density housing areas should be located by existing stations, or new stations should be constructed to serve them. Changes to UK planning guidelines require greater connection between new communities and public transport facilities. Suburban and light rail provision is needed to serve fresh housing, commercial and retail areas. In addition, there should be bus or train linkage so that a maximum walking distance of 400m is achieved. Movement on foot or cycle needs to integrate with public

Table 13.3 Reducing transport CO_2 emissions

– vehicle efficiency improvements
– city traffic management
– improved public transport
– lower speed limits
– encourage journeys on foot or cycle
– remove company car incentives
– integrate land uses
– compact development without zoning

13.7 *Integer House, Watford designed by Cole Thompson. A prototype house that maximises solar gain through a large triple height south facing conservatory (plans (left and top right), section (bottom right) and views opposite page at left)).*

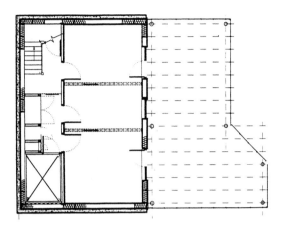

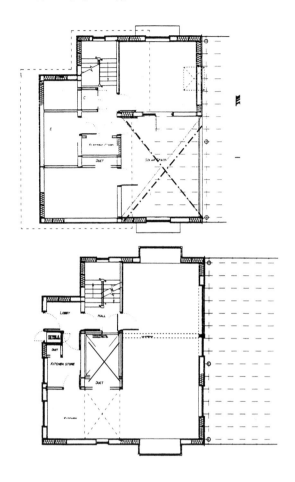

transport facilities with the consequence that stations and trains should provide cycle storage. This is also true of the home where space is required for storing and maintaining bicycles.

Within the lifespan of a typical house (50–100 years) developments in transport technology will alter the relative level of CO_2 efficiencies of different movement modes. Electronic cars may well become as efficient as electronic trains for short journeys. It is important, therefore, that four principles are followed in housing estates:

- site layout should reduce the demand for journeys by integrating land uses
- site density should be such that journey lengths are reduced
- a range of attractive movement modes are provided, with priority given to journeys on foot and cycle
- safety should be a priority through the provision of pedestrian lighting, traffic calming and CCTV.

It is clear that density offers many advantages – energy

13.8 *Layout of Sun Village (Solbyn) near Lund, Sweden by Krister Wiberg. All the houses face south, the school is to the right.*

13.9 *Within the lifetime of new houses photovoltaic technology will become affordable. Southern roof scopes are essential if renewable solar energy is to be exploited (bottom right).*

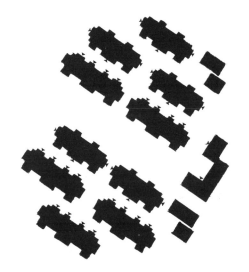

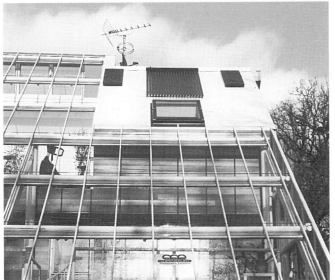

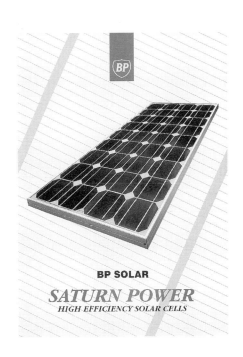

The future

saving, better transportation, safety and security, community ethos – but excessive density of layout can have disadvantages. For instance, high density coupled with poor design can result in an increase in crime and social alienation. High density too can reduce the sense of 'liveability' of public areas and lead to anonymous building design. As density rises, greater tolerance of other people's noise or antisocial behaviour is needed. Finally, high density makes the creation of wildlife areas difficult and undermines attempts to harness energy or rainfall for practical

Table 13.5 Energy use by house type

Type	kWh/yr	Extra cost
Average older house	5,000	—
Average modern house	3,000	—
Super-insulated modern house	1,800	£70/m²
Autonomous house	100-200	£175-200/m²

Source: BRE and DETR Best Practice Reports

Table 13.4 Implications of density for sustainable housing: comparison of three paradigms

Type	Houses/hectare	Advantages	Disadvantages
Low density	10	• renewable energy can readily be exploited • rainwater and greywater systems can be employed • food production in gardens • high biodiversity • high tranquillity	• poor land utilasation • infrastructure costs high • high transport energy costs • high building energy costs unless renewables used
Medium density	30	• renewable energy can be exploited • some local food and energy crops can be grown in gardens • movement by bicycle viable • community greywater systems possible	• public transport will need large subsidy • careful design needed to exploit renewable energy • neighbour disputes can occur over waste or recycling initiatives • poor urban form
High density	60	• compact forms are energy efficient • supports mixed use development • most journeys on foot, bicycle or public transport • good urban design • good microclimate	• crime and vandalism can be a problem • anti-social behaviour undermines community spirit • low tranquility • good design essential • costs can be high per unit

purposes. Without private gardens there is little wildlife or local food production, and as densities increase space for community allotments disappear. Whilst the Broadacre City (1 house per acre) or Garden City (6 houses per acre) ideas are no longer compatible with transport energy costs, there are limits to the density of housing areas if sustainability is to be achieved.[3]

Technical factors in energy efficient housing design

The sustainable house offers enhanced comfort, lower energy or water bills, greater self reliance, improved health, and a more harmonious relationship with nature, seasons and daily cycles. Utopian it may be, but the sustainable house of the future combines spiritual values with good building science. Three factors in particular are emerging as essential construction requirements of the sustainable house:

- thickness of perimeter fabric
- airtightness linked to high levels of insulation
- efficient boiler systems.

They are related and need to be considered as aspects of integrated design for the low energy house.[4] The three factors represent key issues for the designer or developer and relate directly to material choices, energy strategies and lifecycle upgrading of housing.

The Building Research Establishment (BRE) through its arm BRECSU has sought recently to focus attention upon the three topics in order to demonstrate that via an integrated package of fabric, heating and ventilation measures, low energy housing can be achieved at little or no additional cost.

Fabric issues

It is important that in making fabric choices the quality of workmanship is considered. Research suggests that over elaborate detailing or lack of attention to the construction process results in substandard workmanship with conse-

quent cold bridging or moisture penetration. An ideal solution on the drawing board may not result in ideal construction when the realities of the building site are taken into consideration. However, it is worth summarising the current judgement on best practice[5]

- solid floors are relatively easy to insulate to a high standard
- timber floors may cause problems with thermal bridging and moisture transfer
- roofs are easy to insulate to a high standard but poor installation can cause problems
- insulated roofs create warm spaces inside the building envelope for services (this is better than insulated services)
- thickness is important in masonry walls to achieve effective insulation and protection from driving rain
- thermal bridging and moisture remain problems with timber frame construction especially where workmanship cannot be guaranteed.

The question of fabric choice often revolves around the masonry wall - its thickness, materials employed, position and dimensions of insulation. Cavity walls are commonly employed for housing and of three main types of construction the cost varies as follows:[6]

- lightweight block is more expensive than concrete block with extra insulation
- full fill is cheaper than partial fill
- block and render is cheapest.

However, there is uncertainty over the desirability of fully filling the cavity with insulation especially in locations where driving rain occurs. Water penetration across the cavity is not only a fabric problem for the interior but soaked insulation fails to perform its heat retention role and with some insulation materials there is loss of rigidity when wet. Common detail problems that exacerbate driving rain penetration are: recessed mortar joints; flush sills; lack of overhangs at eaves and verges; and blocked weep holes. In exposed situations, the traditional brick outer leaf is not an effective rain barrier even with sound construction. An extra rain shield may be needed, such as a render course or the use of vegetative protection (creepers).

Technical factors alone should not drive design thinking. The thick masonry wall has aesthetic as well as practical advantages. The perception of shelter afforded by the feeling of thickness, especially when combined with modern smaller windows (the result of recent changes to the Building Regulations) results in housing of strong visual character. In other parts of Europe the thick, non brick masonry wall forms the main element of domestic construction. Usually built of rendered concrete block with a wide fully filled insulated cavity, the houses and apartments have an aesthetic robustness often lacking in brick-built Britain. When painted, sometimes as in Berlin or Rotterdam in bright colours, the rendered concrete walls provide a cheerful backcloth to housing areas.

Thermal bridges commonly occur in cavity construction, particularly with poorly specified wall ties or accidental mortar fill. The choice of wall ties is important: steel ties can increase the U value by 6% whilst plastic ties have a negligible impact. With wide cavity construction the wall tie choice is particularly important since with full cavity insulation, the tie is a significant source of heat transfer between the two leaves.

Points to consider if U levels approaching 0.2 W/m²K are to be achieved:

- ensure there is good contact between wall and roof insulation at the eaves. Ventilate outside the insulated envelope
- ensure there is good contact between floor and wall insulation at the base of the wall. Use lightweight blocks for the lower course if necessary and turn up insulation
- the detailing of window and door frames is important if cold bridging is to be avoided
- steel lintels, even when insulated, can cause cold bridging. Separate lintels are best with a proprietary cavity closer
- fully filled wide cavities can be used in severe climates with wall ties available for cavities up to 300mm wide.

So far the concentration has been on traditional masonry construction (brick or concrete block) but timber and steel framing offers many potential benefits for sustainable housing. As long as it is obtained from a certified forest source, timber construction is a particularly sustainable form of building. It is not only low in embodied energy, but the tree is an effective converter of CO_2 to oxygen. However, there are three main drawbacks to the use of timber frame construction in sustainable housing:

- timber is a relatively good conductor and hence in the super-insulated wall the elements of the timber frame significantly reduce energy performance
- timber is generally more expensive than masonry construction, but offers greater speed of erection and enhanced quality control
- moisture penetration in the wall or roof can occur as a result of poor design or construction. Interstitial condensation is a particular problem especially if the vapour barrier is poorly installed or becomes damaged.

Brick is often used as an external rain screen in timber frame construction but there needs to be a ventilated cavity to allow any moisture to dry out. At the inner face of the wall it is important that airtightness is achieved to avoid moisture laden air passing into the construction. The position, type and integrity of the air/vapour barrier is crucial to avoid moisture collecting in concealed areas of the wall where wet or dry rot could go undetected. Double vapour barriers are needed of different resistance (by a factor of 5 to 1) to control moisture diffusion in the fabric.

Irrespective of technical difficulties, timber framing offers many potential benefits for sustainable housing. In a period of skill and material shortage, the industrialisation and waste minimalisation of timber house prefabrication is useful. Productivity per man is high and by using kits there is a high measure of customer choice. In Japan, where the housing market is about eight times that in the UK, about half of all new housing (apartment and detached) is constructed by timber frame means.[7] If current problems of moisture control, airtightness and customer conservatism can be overcome, timber framed housing could be the key to a more sustainable future in Britain.

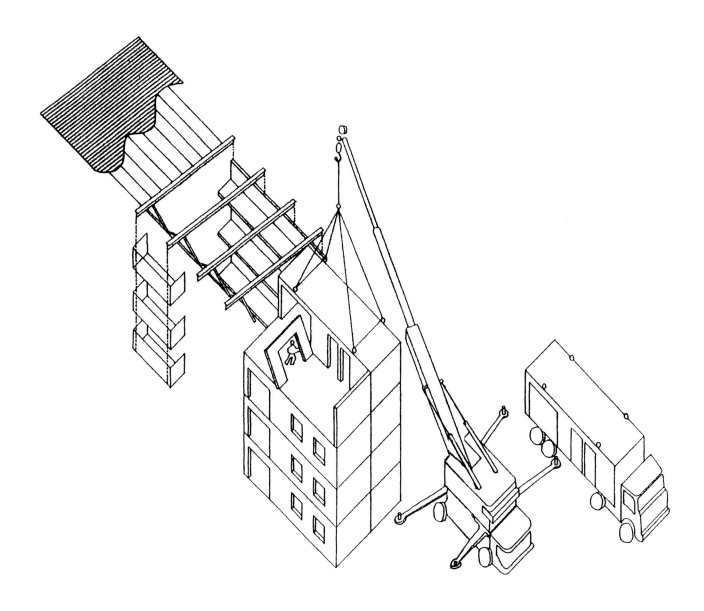

An example in the UK is a group of 12 houses designed by Architype for the Greenwich Self-Build Co-operative at Thamesmead. Using a timber frame incorporating structural I beams and locally sourced Douglas Fir cladding, the highly insulated houses achieved U values of around 0.2 W/m²Kin the walls resulting in anticipated heating bills of only £30–50 per year.[8] Such performance suggests that, if consumer resistance can be overcome, the present level of only 7% of new houses in Britain exploiting timber frame technologies could be greatly increased.

Steel framing too looks set to increase its market penetration in UK housing. Like timber framing, the steel framed house takes advantage of greater quality control through factory production and enhanced speed of construction. Greater speed cuts site overheads resulting in a potential cost saving to the builder of £2,000 per house.[9] The precision of steel has aesthetic as well as technical advantages and since half of all new steel in the UK consists of recycled steel, there are green arguments in the material's favour.

As in masonry construction, airtightness is important in achieving a highly insulated wall and in controlling moisture penetration. Leakage of air is often hard to detect but can account for significant heat loss (see later). New

13.11 *Key benefits of efficient ventilation. BRE/Brian Edwards*

13.12 *Passive solar water heaters on southern roof slopes in sheltered housing near Davis, California (opposite).*

Table 13.6 Comparison of cost and speed of construction (based upon TRADA, Timber Frame 2,000 Project)

Material	Structural frame cost £/m²	Site production m² per week
Timber	58	656
Steel	79	909
Masonry	61	333

See also *Building Design*, 20 November 1998, p. 20-1

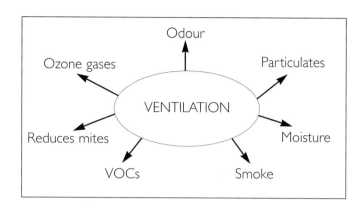

forms of construction for use in sustainable housing such as the steel stud frame can offer advantages in terms of recycling, quality control, speed of erection and prefabrication. At the opposite extreme, earth sheltering and straw bale construction provide possible solutions in certain situations. In both cases ecological principles linked to waste, shelter and reduced environmental footprint suggest that demonstration projects are needed at this stage rather than volume housing.

Airtightness

The highly insulated house needs to pay particular attention to air infiltration and ventilation. Unless they are well controlled, infiltration and ventilation can be the main source of heat loss for the super-insulated house.[10] Infiltration is the unintended ingress of cold air into the house and egress of warm air out of it. Ventilation is the intentional movement of both. Air leakage is the term used to measure ventilation, especially when using pressure tests.

Ventilation in the home is important to:

- maintain healthy conditions for occupants
- control humidity (and hence combat condensation)
- reduce dust mite populations (and the risk of asthma attacks)
- disperse pollution from combustion or fabric emissions.

In modern homes dust mites are a major threat to health and comfort. It has been estimated by the BRE that in poorly ventilated, modern carpeted houses, there may be as many as 14,000 dust mites per square metre of floor, and that 10% of the weight of feather filled pillows or duvets may be mites and their droppings. Since the house dust mite thrives in high moisture environments, the key is enhanced ventilation. Lowering the moisture content of the air quickly and cheaply reduces dust mite populations. Enhanced ventilation also tackles other health or amenity problems in the home. But ventilation is a major source of heat loss and hence the type and design of ventilation is important. The key to good ventilation is control.

Unwanted ventilation is a common problem especially in older houses where unwanted air movement can be equivalent to having a window 0.6m² permanently open. In new construction it is possible to achieve high levels of airtightness with controlled ventilation, thereby achieving good levels of energy efficiency. In masonry construction, low airleakage rates can be obtained by fully filling cavities, sealing openings (especially around service pipes) and by using wet plaster on the inside and cement render on the outside.[11] In timber frame construction, good airtightness can be achieved by careful detailing of the vapour control barrier, external sheathing and breather paper, especially around service penetrations.

Airtightness is often a function of the method of ventilation. With natural systems based upon trickle vents,

opening windows and stack ventilation, the performance varies according to external conditions and user preference. Opening windows, though fairly cheap and popular, are a common source of house burglaries. Mechanical ventilation consists of extract fans, room ventilators with heat recovery and whole house systems with heat recovery.[12] They offer fine control over ventilation but can be noisy and expensive to run although they recover up to 90% of the extracted heat. A new system available to designers is called passive stack ventilation (PSV) which adjusts the amount of ventilation according to moisture levels present in the air. It is particularly useful in kitchens and bathrooms where temperature gradients drive the system without extract fans.

Airtightness needs to be part of the initial design strategy for the house. Simple measures are often effective, such as the avoidance of built-in joists (joist hangers are best), the use of wet plaster rather than dry lining, the effective sealing between elements of construction, making one person (or trade) responsible on site for airtightness, and designing for ventilation (rather than letting it happen).

Heating systems

The highly insulated, airtight house requires the same level of design care given to the heating and hot water system. New technologies and improvements to old ones have greatly expanded the choices available in the domestic sector. In terms of central heating boilers, choose a low water content boiler with a lighter heat exchanger, efficient burners and a modulating gas and air supply.[13] It is also important to avoid permanent pilot boilers especially in highly insulated airtight houses.

In the low energy house the boiler will not often be on because casual gains (solar, cooking, people, lights, etc.) may be sufficient for space heating for much of the year. If the controls are not adequate there may be overheating, and ideally there should be both radiator thermostatic controls and house thermostats. In the super-insulated house the boiler's main task is to provide hot water, not space heating. Over the year the energy use for hot water exceeds that for heating in modern efficient homes.

It makes a lot of sense to pre-heat the cold water (by

using passive solar water heaters, see Figure 13.12) and to avoid locating the cold water tank in the unheated roof-space. Hot water can be supplied directly from a combi-type boiler but although it is cheap to install and run, there are limits to capacity that restrict combi boilers to small houses.

The average heating load for a super-insulated three bedroom semi-detached house is around one kilowatt and less for a modern well insulated terraced house. Full central heating may not be the best solution here and separate room heaters can offer economies of cost and fuel bills. However, the picture is complex and besides cost, it is important to consider CO_2 emissions, moisture levels, the opportunity for heat recovery, water use and flueing arrangements. The sustainable house has to be healthy as well as comfortable and cheap to run. But as houses have their ventilation controlled and their level of insulation improved, heating can be provided as a by-product of other services in the home (such as lighting, cooking and the hot water system).

In conclusion, every decision affects energy consumption – site planning, level of occupation, services choice, airtightness, glazing area, daylighting levels, passive solar, insulation levels and fabric choice. Each decision also affects air quality and the feeling of well-being that the house gives. To be truly sustainable, housing of the future must offer more than low energy design – it needs to provide for healthy lifestyles in socially enriching communities.

Sustainable housing: relating energy and health

The causal links between energy consumption, housing condition and occupant health are generally well established.[14] Cold, damp and poorly ventilated dwellings lead to both high levels of energy usage and to human health problems, mainly in the form of asthma, bronchitis and arthritic ailments. When retrofitting dwellings it is important that the impact upon health is given due weighting - particularly bearing in mind the likely level of fuel poverty present and the generally poor lifestyles of many in public sector housing. It is estimated that the financial burden upon the National Health Service for asthma related illnesses is in excess of £1 billion a year, and although urban air quality is a cause, the internal condition of many dwellings is a major contributor.

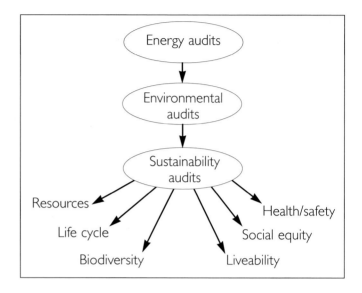

The correlation between dampness and a range of medical complaints is well established as is that between internal temperatures and winter deaths. The full cost of illness associated with poor housing is difficult to quantify but with the health and work related costs taken together it is probably about 25% of all the money spent in the UK on home heating. The National Asthma Campaign estimated that over three million people are affected by the condition, many children being amongst the most chronic sufferers. Asthma accounts for about 18 million working days lost in the UK annually and over 10 million school days lost.

Dust mites are a significant agent in the asthma condition. Cold, damp, inadequately ventilated housing creates the ideal conditions for dust mite colonisation. The drive towards energy efficiency has, in fact, contributed to the expansion in dust mite populations – especially in existing dwellings. Moisture balance is critical for the dust mite which prefers a relative humidity of around 80% and an internal temperature in the range of 21–25°C. These are the very conditions created by many of the energy efficiency measures undertaken over the past few years, such as double glazing, ventilation control, enhanced insulation, and the move from open fires to sealed heating systems.

Refurbishment needs, therefore, to consider not just the reduction in energy costs but the consequences upon the internal environment from the point of view of health. There are several interrelated factors: heating; ventilation; size of rooms; method of clothes washing; type of construction; and lifestyle. Architects are responsible for only some of these factors, so refurbishment (and new build) requires a team approach embracing user, client, energy supplier and perhaps community health representative. Taking each issue in isolation is likely to lead to only a partial solution to community renewal through housing refurbishment (Figure 13.14).

The SAP rating system

In 1993 the UK government introduced a standard system for home energy rating. Known as the Standard Assessment Procedure (SAP) it is based on the BRE's domestic energy model (BREDEM). It provides a simple and nationally consistent means of estimating the energy performance of new or refurbished dwellings. SAP ratings are expressed on a scale of 1–100 and relate to standards in the Building Regulations. The DETR encourages all those involved in housing provision (professional groups, housing associations, local authorities, mortgage companies) to use SAP ratings as a means of assessing energy efficiency.

There is a simple methodology behind the SAP system based upon type of construction, window type and area, level of insulation, orientation, size of dwelling, ventilation rate, method of heating etc. The rating is intended to be a guide and to highlight the different potential performance of housing available to home buyers or tenants. The higher the rating, the better the energy efficiency of the dwelling. The system is comparative and allows houses to be compared before and after improvement, and between one house type and another. It is a useful tool for designers in highlighting the importance of energy efficient design to clients.

Hockerton Energy Project

The Hockerton Energy Project in Nottinghamshire is a small demonstration scheme designed by Robert and Brenda Vale and built by Nick Martin who was the contractor involved in the Vale's autonomous house. It consists of a parallel row of south facing, earth sheltered terraced houses. The project integrates a number of key low energy and ecological considerations. Water, for instance, is locally gathered, cleaned and used as greywater for certain domestic functions.

The construction is highly rational: a series of structural crosswalls that brace the retaining wall (of the earth sheltered element) and act as a heat store for the passive solar gains. The design approach differentiates between primary and secondary low energy strategies, thereby bringing the interaction between cost, buildability and environmental factors into clearer focus. Considerable attention is paid to the connections between insulation, fabric and glazing systems with the result that triple glazing, unusual in medium cost housing, is justified.

Table 13.7 Key elements of the autonomous house

Energy	– biomass
	– wind
	– solar
	– geo-thermal
Water	– roof collection
	– recycling of grey water
	– local treatment (reed beds)
Waste	– compost
	– energy extraction
	– separation

Table 13.8 Main features of Hockerton Energy Village

- earth sheltering construction
- orientation for solar gain
- wide frontage, shallow plan terraced layout
- plot width south facing conservatory
- domestic water collection from conservatory roof
- zero CO_2 emissions and 100% water self-sufficiency
- double glazed conservatory
- triple glazed internal windows
- 300mm insulation

Table 13.9 Key targets of Hockerton Energy Housing Project

- 90% energy saving compared with conventional house
- self-sufficient in water
- EU bathing water standard of sewerage effluent from site
- 3 month temperature time lag due to earth sheltering
- 70% heat recovery from extracted warmed air
- one fossil-fuelled car per household
- 100% self-sufficiency in fruit, vegetables and dairy products using organic/permaculture principles
- 8 hour per person per week in support activities

Source: Hockerton Housing Project: Key facts

The Hockerton Energy Project is part of an important collection of experiments in sustainable housing north of Nottingham. Besides Hockerton and the Vale's House at Southwell, plans are afoot to create a substantial low energy estate at the nearby Sherwood Energy Park and to develop CHP schemes using locally grown biomass in former mining villages around Ollerton. These and other projects are the initiative of the Newark and Sherwood Energy Agency, partly funded by the European Union.

Table 13.10 Five conditions for sustainable housing

• Low resource use	– energy
	– water
	– other resources (land, minerals, etc)
• Safe	– security through design
• Healthy	– physical health
	– mental health (stress)
• Productive	– socially
	– economically
• Beautiful	– aesthetically
	– spiritually
	– ecologically

References

1. *Building a Sustainable Future: Homes for an Autonomous Community* General Information Report 53, DETR, 1998.
2. Ibid, p. 6.
3. Ibid, p. 8.
4. *Advanced Housing Seminar: Integrated Design in New UK Housing* Seminar Proceedings, BRECSU, 1998, p. 12.
5. This section is based upon *Fabric Issues* by Peter Warm in *BRECSU Proceedings* cited above.
6. Ibid.
7. Barrie Evans, "Learning from the Japanese", *The Architects' Journal*, 19 November 1998, p. 60.
8. *Building Design* 'Housing Technical Supplement', 20 November 1998, p21.
9. Ibid, p. 20.
10. *Airtightness and Ventilation* by Howard Atkin in *BRECSU Proceedings* cited above.
11. Ibid.
12. *Heating and Hot Water Systems* by John Willoughby in *BRECSU Proceedings*, p. 12.
13. Ibid, p. 14. See also Willoughby, J., Swann, B. and Warm, P. (1998) "Innovative Energy and Environmental Heating Technologies in UK Housing" *Proc CIBSE National Conference*.
14. See for instance Stirling Howieson and Alan Lawson "Who is Paying the Fuel Price" *Environment by Design*, Autumn 1998, Vol 2, Number 2, pp. 139–152.

13.15 *Plan, section and perspective sketch of Hockerton Energy Project, Nottinghamshire, showing the various low energy strategies.*
Architects: Robert and Brenda Vale

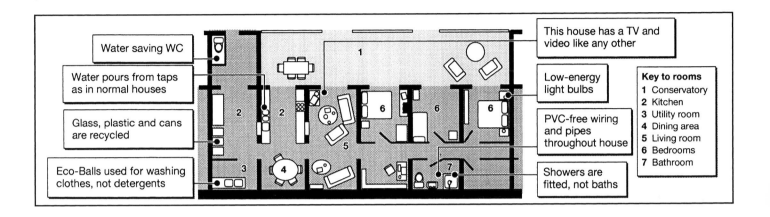

Water saving WC

Water pours from taps as in normal houses

Glass, plastic and cans are recycled

Eco-Balls used for washing clothes, not detergents

This house has a TV and video like any other

Low-energy light bulbs

PVC-free wiring and pipes throughout house

Showers are fitted, not baths

Key to rooms
1 Conservatory
2 Kitchen
3 Utility room
4 Dining area
5 Living room
6 Bedrooms
7 Bathroom

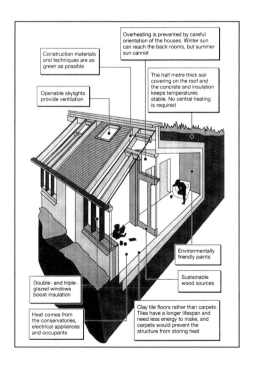

Overheating is prevented by careful orientation of the houses. Winter sun can reach the back rooms, but summer sun cannot

Construction materials and techniques are as green as possible

The half metre thick soil covering on the roof and the concrete and insulation keeps temperatures stable. No central heating is required

Openable skylights provide ventilation

Environmentally friendly paints

Sustainable wood sources

Double- and triple-glazed windows boost insulation

Heat comes from the conservatories, electrical appliances and occupants

Clay tile floors rather than carpets. Tiles have a longer lifespan and need less energy to make, and carpets would prevent the structure from storing heat

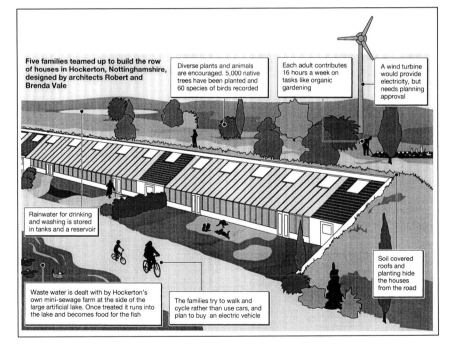

Five families teamed up to build the row of houses in Hockerton, Nottinghamshire, designed by architects Robert and Brenda Vale

Diverse plants and animals are encouraged. 5,000 native trees have been planted and 60 species of birds recorded

Each adult contributes 16 hours a week on tasks like organic gardening

A wind turbine would provide electricity, but needs planning approval

Rainwater for drinking and washing is stored in tanks and a reservoir

Waste water is dealt with by Hockerton's own mini-sewage farm at the side of the large artificial lake. Once treated it runs into the lake and becomes food for the fish

The families try to walk and cycle rather than use cars, and plan to buy an electric vehicle

Soil covered roofs and planting hide the houses from the road

Select Bibliography

Reports

Building a Sustainable Future: Homes for an Autonomous Community General Information Report 53, DETR.

Sustainable Development: The UK Strategy, HMSO, 1994.

Opportunities for Change: Consultation paper on a UK strategy for sustainable construction, HMSO, 1998.

The Green Guide to Specification: Building Research Establishment, 1999.

Review of Ultra-low-energy Homes, BRECSU, 1998.

Passive Solar Estate Layout, BRECSU, 1997.

Books

Calthorpe, P. The Next American Metropolis, Princeton University Press, 1993.

Edwards, B. *Sustainable Architecture*, Architectural Press, 1999.

Energy Conscious Design: A Primer for Architects, Batsford for the Commission of the European Communities, 1992.

Girardet, H. *The Gaia Atlas of Cities: New Directions for Sustainable Urban Living*, Gaia Books, 1992.

Jenks, M., Burton, E. and Williams, K. *The Compact City: A Sustainable Urban Form?* E & FN Spon, 1996.

Rogers, R. *Cities for a Small Planet*, Faber & Faber, 1997.

Rudin, D. and Falk, R. *Building the 21st Century Home: The sustainable urban neighbourhood*, Architectural Press, 1999.

Urban Task Force. *Towards an Urban Renaissance*, E & FN Spon, 1999.

Vale, B. and R. *Green Architecture: Design for a Sustainable Future* Thames & Hudson, 1991.

Woolley, T., Kimmins, S. and Harrison, R. *Green Building Handbook*, E & FN Spon, 1997.

Index

First published 2000 by E & FN Spon
11 New Fetter Lane, London EC4P 4EE

Simultaneously published in the USA and Canada
by E & FN Spon, an imprint of Routledge
29 West 35th Street, New York, NY 10001

E & FN Spon is an imprint of the Taylor & Francis Group

© 2000 Brian Edwards and David Turrent

Typeset in Gill Sans by Stephen Cary

Printed and bound in Great Britain

British Library Cataloguing in Publication Data
A catalogue record for this book is available from the British Library

Library of Congress Cataloguing in Publication Data
Sustainable housing: priciples and practice / [edited by] Brian Edwards
and David Turrent.
p. cm.
Includes bibliographical references (p.)
1. Housing - Great Britain. 2. Sustainable development - Great Britain.
I. Edwards, Brian, MSc. II. Turrent, D.
HD7333.A3S847 2000
363.5'8'0941 - dc21 99-36151

ISBN 0-419-24620-7

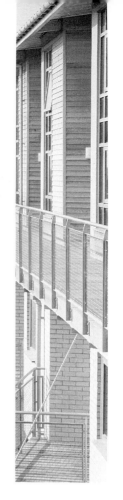

Brian Edwards and David Turrent

Sustainable Housing
Principles & Practice

London and New York